The Developmentally Responsive Middle Level Principal: A Leadership Model and Measurement Instrument

Vincent A. Anfara, Jr.

Kathleen Roney

Claudia Smarkola

Joseph P. DuCette

Steven J. Gross

National Middle School Association

Westerville, Ohio

National Middle School Association
4151 Executive Parkway, Suite 300
Westerville, Ohio 43081
www.nmsa.org

Sue Swaim, Executive Director
Jeff Ward, Deputy Executive Director
Edward Brazee, Editor, Professional Publications
John Lounsbury, Consulting Editor, Professional Publications
April Tibbles, Director of Publications
Mary Mitchell, Designer, Editorial Assistant
Dawn Williams, Production Specialist
Mark Shumaker, Graphic Designer
Lisa Snyder, Graphic Designer
Cheri Howman, Proofreader
Marcia Meade-Hurst, Senior Publications Representative

Library of Congress Cataloging-in-Publication Data
The developmentally responsive middle level principal: a leadership model and measurement instrument/Vincent A. Anfara, Jr .... [et al.].
        p. cm.
    Includes bibliographical references.
    ISBN 1-56090-194-2 (pbk.)
    1. Middle school principals.   2. Middle schools--Administration.   3. Leadership.
Anfara, Vincent A.
LB2822.5.D48 2006
373.12'012--dc22

                2006048127

Contents

Acknowledgements

We are indebted to the following middle schools and principals who cooperated in the development of the Middle Level Leadership Questionnaire (MLLQ):

Cedar Bluff Middle School, Knoxville, TN	Clifford Davis, Jr.
Holston Middle School, Knoxville, TN	Thomas L. Brown
Arcola Middle School, Norristown, PA	John A. Bravo
Charles F. Patton Middle School, Kennett Square, PA	Bruce H. Vosburgh
Ridley Middle School, Ridley Park, PA	Gail L. Heinemeyer
Stoddard-Fleisher Middle School, Philadelphia, PA	Thomas R. Davidson

and

Three middle schools and principals who requested to remain anonymous.

Thanks are also extended to:

Robert B. Gratz, coordinator of middle schools, Knox County, Knoxville, TN

The middle school principals of Knox County, Knoxville, TN

The officers and board of trustees of the Tennessee Association of Middle Schools

Introduction

Almost all educational reform reports have come to the conclusion that the nation cannot attain excellence in education without effective school leadership.
— Crawford, 1998, p. 8

Twenty-two years after the initial release of *This We Believe* (NMSA, 1982), the National Middle School Association in *This We Believe: Successful Schools for Young Adolescents* (2003) formally recognized the need for courageous and collaborative leadership by including it as one of the 14 characteristics of successful middle schools.

Educators know that effective school leaders: (1) recognize teaching and learning as the main business of school; (2) communicate the school's mission and vision clearly and consistently to all constituents; (3) promote an atmosphere of trust and collaboration; and (4) emphasize high-quality, focused, and sustained professional development (see Bauck, 1987; George & Grebing, 1992; Weller, 1999). Despite the consensus that leadership counts, deep philosophical and political disagreements persist about what kind of educational leaders are needed; what knowledge, skills, and dispositions they should possess; and how they should be professionally prepared and developed.

Some researchers (Barnard, 1938; Schön, 1987) have argued that part of being effective is having the ability to be self-reflective and identify strengths and weaknesses and the discrepancies between actions and beliefs in order to improve the quality of one's work as a leader. Other researchers (Bernhardt, 1998; Stack, 2003) have added into the mix of what is required to be an effective school leader the ability to collect, analyze, and use data for the explicit purpose of school improvement. This book is dedicated to both of these processes: being self-reflective *and* effectively using data, specifically data pertaining to the effectiveness of the principal as part of that self-reflection for professional growth and development. Ultimately, all of these efforts are aimed at overall school improvement. The essential question addressed in this book is: *As a middle level principal, am I developmentally responsive to the needs of young adolescents, their teachers, and the school itself?* But before we consider how to answer that question, a look at the issues related to data-driven decision making and reflective practice is in order. The introduction will be concluded by reviewing what we know about the middle level principal.

Gathering and Analyzing Data

Data-driven decision making has been defined as the "consistent use of objective information to enhance human judgment" (Jandris, 2001). Data "identify the link between educational practices and student performance so that high achievement levels can be obtained" (Miller, 2000). According to Wade (2001)

> When systematically collected and analyzed, data provide an accurate way of identifying problem areas in school programs. Data reveal strengths and weaknesses in students' knowledge and skills, and they provide meaningful guidance on how teaching practices can and should be altered. When acknowledged and accepted by a faculty, data can lead to the formulation and implementation of corrective courses of action that can solve problems and meet the school's goals. (p. 2)

What types of data are most useful in school contexts? Answers found in the literature include

- Student assessment data including measurements of student performance, such as standardized test results and grade point averages
- Student demographic data such as enrollment, attendance, grade level, ethnicity, gender, socioeconomic status, language proficiency, and student mobility rates
- Perception data obtained from surveys, questionnaires, and interviews with teachers, administrators, parents, students, and community members
- School program data that define and describe programs, instructional strategies, and classroom practices.

Remember what we noted in the first sentence of this monograph—"...the nation cannot attain excellence in education without effective school leadership." Where are the data that need to be collected on the effectiveness of the school principal? Anfara, Patterson, Buehler, and Gearity (2004) noted in their study of school improvement planning that data related to principals were simply not collected in any of 16 middle schools studied. Data must be collected on the principal's effectiveness and these data should be used both for school improvement and for the principal's professional development. Principals should be keenly interested in their effectiveness as instructional leaders, their ability to function as collaborative decision makers, or most specifically their ability to be developmentally responsive.

Unlike most organizations and businesses, schools have been able to operate pretty effectively in the past without critically using

> Principals should be keenly interested in their effectiveness as instructional leaders, their ability to function as collaborative decision makers, or most specifically their ability to be developmentally responsive.

data. However, the accountability and standards movement has forced schools to become much more data-driven and results-oriented. In addition to using data to identify root causes of achievement problems in the school, the school improvement process creates the opportunity for school leaders to use research and effective practices to help set improvement goals. There is a willingness to use the best available research to inform practice. Virtually every school improvement process at the state level requires school leaders to use research and best available practices as the knowledge base for school improvement goals.

Using data in decision making is not a new idea. But there are many issues that impede the use of this information in decision making due to the political nature of schooling, the lack of consensus on educational goals, and the inexperience of many educators with using data. In the case of the school principal, there is no question that allowing oneself to be publicly evaluated can be a threatening proposition.

Schools have always been somewhat ambivalent about the role of data in education. On the one hand, schools generate an abundance of information. On the other hand, schools have never been quite certain what to do with all this information. Traditionally, school leaders have satisfied their data obligations by filing the required forms and moving on to the next task. Seldom have they actually been expected to use the data in making decisions that could benefit student achievement. Now more than ever, principals are being asked to use data in reflecting on their practice and use this information for potential professional development opportunities.

State accountability systems and the recently reauthorized Elementary and Secondary Education Act (ESEA) have forced schools to consider ways that data can be used for guiding school improvement. Moreover, No Child Left Behind requires that schools disaggregate the data by ethnicity, disability, gender, socioeconomic level, migrant status, and English proficiency. Clearly, schools need the capacity to extract, report on, and use a wide range of information. That wide variety of information should include data related to the principal and his or her effectiveness.

> Allowing oneself to be publicly evaluated can be a threatening proposition.

To highlight the distinctive nature of data-driven decision making, Table 1 (p. 4) is offered. The left-hand column provides the characteristics of the kind of decision making we were accustomed to before the major emphasis on school accountability. The right-hand column reflects the shift in thinking that is essential for data-driven decision making in schools.

Although using data is not a panacea for solving every school problem, when properly used, data can raise student educational achievement and increase confidence among faculty, students, parents, and the community. And data focused on the principal's effectiveness will significantly help principals interested in improving their practice.

Table 1
Types of Decision Making

Decision Making Based on Intuition, Tradition, or Convenience	Data-Driven Decision Making
Scattered staff development programs	Focused staff development program as an improvement strategy to address documented problems/needs
Budgetary decisions based on prior practice and/or priority programs	Budget allocations to programs based on data-informed needs
Staff assignments based on interest and availability	Staff assignments based on skills needed, as indicated by the data
Reports to the community about school events	Organized factual reports to the community about the learning progress of students
Goal setting by board members, administrators, or teachers based on votes, favorite initiatives, or fads	Goal setting based on data about problems and possible explanations
Staff meetings that focus on operations and the dissemination of information	Staff meetings that focus on strategies and issues raised by the school's data
Parent/family communication via semiannual conferences and newsletters	Regular parent/family communication regarding the progress of their children
Grading system based on each teacher's criteria of completed work and participation	Grading system based on common criteria for student performance that reports progress on the standards as well as work skills
Periodic administrative team meetings focused on operations	Administrative team meetings that focus on measured progress toward data-based improvement goals

Adapted from North Central Regional Educational Laboratory (2000). *Using data to bring about positive results in school improvement efforts.*

The Principal as Reflective Practitioner

Theory and research together is only one source of knowledge. Another source is knowledge gained through practice. Reflective practice is based on the reality that professional knowledge is different from scientific knowledge. Professional knowledge is created through experience as professionals face ill-defined, unique, and challenging problems and set courses of action. The late Ralph Tyler maintained that researchers don't have a full understanding of the nature of professional knowledge in education.

> Researchers and many academics also misunderstand educational practices. The practice of every profession evolves informally, and professional procedures are not generally derived from systematic design based on research findings. Professional practice has largely developed through trial and error and intuitive efforts. Practitioners, through the years, discover procedures that appear to work and others that fail.
>
> (cited in Hosford, 1984, p. 9)

From Tyler's perspective, scientific studies are important because they explain phenomenon, but they do not produce practice. Educational practitioners rely heavily on informed intuition as they create knowledge through experience. Intuition is informed both by theoretical knowledge and by interacting with the context of practice. When principals use informed intuition, they too are engaging in reflective practice. Schön (1983) suggested,

> They may ask themselves, for example, what features do I notice when I recognize this thing? What are the criteria by which I make this judgment? What procedures am I enacting when I perform this skill? How am I framing the problem that I'm trying to solve? Usually, reflection on knowing-in-action goes together with reflection on the stuff at hand. There is some puzzling, or troubling or interesting phenomenon with which the individual is trying to deal. As he tries to make sense of it, he also reflects on the understandings which have been implicit in his action, understandings which he surfaces, criticizes, re-structures and embodies in further action. It is this process of reflection-in-action which is central to the "art" by which practitioners sometimes deal with situations of uncertainty, instability, uniqueness, and value conflicts. (p. 50)

Reflection-in-action captures the principal at work as he or she makes judgments in trying to manage a very messy work context.

The key to reflective practice can be found in the famous psychologist William James' 1892 message to the teachers of Cambridge, Massachusetts. He pointed out the importance of "an intermediary inventive mind" in making practical application of scientific knowledge. In his words,

The science of logic never made a man reason rightly, and the science of ethics…never made a man behave rightly. The most such science can do is help us catch ourselves up and check ourselves, if we start to reason or behave wrongly; and to criticize ourselves more articulately after we make mistakes. A science only lays down lines within which the rules of the art must fall, laws which the follower of the art must not transgress; but what particular thing he shall positively do within those lines is left exclusively to his own genius. (p. 8)

Central to the idea of reflection is the identification of discrepancies between beliefs and actions—by reflecting on these discrepancies, school administrators can identify ways to improve the quality of their work. Educational beliefs are shaped by past experiences with parents, mentors, and other role models. Through the reflective process, it is possible to discover that actions are the result of beliefs—some that are examined and some that are not. Discovery of the beliefs that drive actions enables the reflective practitioner to modify actions to ensure they are consistent with professional beliefs. This process leads to information about one's philosophy; leadership capacity; commitment to professional growth; ability to anticipate problems, develop alternatives, and take risks; and willingness to accept challenging assignments. In short, reflective practice can facilitate both individual and organizational change through contrasting one's actions to the ideal of the practice being examined.

> Reflective practice can facilitate both individual and organizational change through contrasting one's actions to the ideal of the practice being examined.

According to Sergiovanni (2001), the idea of reflective practice is still relatively new, and much more thought needs to be given to its development and use in educational administration. He wrote,

It seems clear, nonetheless, that reflective principals are in charge of their professional practice. They do not passively accept solutions and mechanically apply them. They do not assume that the norm is the one best way to practice, and they are suspicious of easy answers to complex questions. They are painfully aware of how context and situations vary, how teachers and students differ in many ways, and how complex school goals and objectives actually are.… At the same time, reflective professional practice requires that principals have a healthy respect for, be well informed about, and use the best available theory and research and accumulated practice wisdom. (p. 46)

The Middle School Principal

Obviously the principal plays the major role in the development of a successful middle school. We have heard numerous accounts of exemplary middle schools that changed drastically for the worse because of the appointment of a new principal who knows little about the middle school concept or the nature of young adolescents. One would think that because of the importance of the person who holds this position that much research has been done on the middle level principal. Unfortunately, there is a significant lack of research in this area. Much of what exists is descriptive in nature documenting the characteristics of those holding middle school principalships (e.g., age, gender, certification, degree, and the like) and the programs and practices found in middle schools (e.g., teaming, advisory, transition programs).

Key studies include those conducted under the direction of the National Association of Secondary School Principals (NASSP). These studies were conducted by Valentine and associates (1981, 1993, 2002). The most recent *National Study of Leadership in Middle Level Schools* (Valentine, Clark, Hackman, & Petzko, 2002) provided a comprehensive description of the characteristics of middle level principals at the start of the 21st century. One of its noteworthy conclusions is that many of the middle level principals came to the position with little or no prior administrative background and no expertise in middle level issues. In 2004 a follow-up study (Valentine et al.) was conducted that compared this national sample of middle level principals to 98 principals in highly successful schools. Approximately twice as many principals of highly successful schools had majored in middle level education at the master's, specialist, or doctoral level than had their counterparts in the national sample.

In an attempt to give a more complete understanding of the distinctive nature of the middle level principalship, Little and Little (2001) selected a panel of 10 middle level experts to generate a list of essential characteristics. This list contains 59 characteristics including items like "builds confidence and inspires others," "has effective oral, written, listening, and interpersonal skills," "generates enthusiasm," "has a sense of humor," and "energizes the faculty to try innovative ideas" (pp. 4-6). Of the 59 characteristics, only 5 are specific to a middle school principal.

1. Is committed to developmentally responsive middle level education.
2. Is thoroughly knowledgeable about middle level curriculum, programs, and practices.
3. Understands the unique nature of young adolescent learners.
4. Has a commitment to the centrality of the interdisciplinary team organization, and has the skills in scheduling and supervision to make them effective groups.
5. Has a compassionate understanding of the nature and needs of older children and young adolescents. (excerpted from pp. 4-5)

Using the 59 characteristics, Little and Little (2001) developed a "Self-reporting Inventory" for principals and a "Faculty Perceptions of the Middle School Principal's

Effectiveness" survey. While this instrument is extremely useful and helps middle level principals evaluate their practice, it does not move us forward in the development of a model of leadership that is specific to middle schools.

Anfara, Brown, Mills, Hartman, and Mahar (2000), Brown, Anfara, Hartman, Mahar, and Mills (2001), and Anfara and Brown (2003) have conducted a number of qualitative studies on the preparation and professional development of middle level principals. The following two comments of individuals related to their preservice preparation were typical.

> I went through my entire college training program for administration and did not even hear the words "middle school philosophy." I started as a middle school principal and had no idea what exploratory curriculum was, what advisories were, and how to organize teachers into effective, functioning teams.

> Nothing I studied in my preparation program prepared me to work in a middle school. Luckily I was an assistant principal under a principal who had read and studied the middle school concept.

Unfortunately, the assumption is made that because a principal holds an administrative position (i.e., principal of a middle school) that he or she already knows what the principal needs to know, and school districts do not invest much time and resources into their professional development.

When asked about professional development, middle school principals emphasized the need to know more about the nature of the young adolescent and the meaning of the phrase "developmentally appropriate" in relation to curriculum, instruction, assessment, and the organization and structure of a middle school.

It is important that principals have a firm understanding of middle school philosophy, curriculum, and instructional practices.

There is no doubt that if middle grades principals are to promote quality middle schools they must possess basic skills and knowledge in school administration, but it is just as important that they also have a firm understanding of middle school philosophy, curriculum, and instructional practices. In addition to dealing with instructional leadership, participatory management/leadership, school improvement planning, school-based budgeting and financial management, and a host of other issues, middle grades principals must be knowledgeable about young adolescents and what components or structures (e.g., teaming, advisory, exploratories) have been deemed essential for the "successful" middle school (see NMSA, 2003).

Currently, few middle grades principals are specifically prepared to work with young adolescents. Most have not received any formal preparation in the instructional and organizational needs of a middle school. Many do not understand the nature of young adolescents and its relationship to teaching and learning and the everyday functioning of a school. Gaskill (2002) reported that only seven states have special certification programs for middle grades principals. They are Alaska, Kentucky, Massachusetts, Missouri, Nebraska, Ohio, and Oklahoma; but only five of these require the middle level credential. While the number of states that have recognized the need to have middle level administrative licensure is very low, the picture becomes even bleaker when one investigates the content of educational administration programs in these states. In most instances only an internship (field-based experience) is required in a middle school setting. In a few of the seven states there is an additional course or two focused on the educational issues related to young adolescents.

Currently, the trend at the state level is to offer Pre-K-12 administrative licensure. As educational administration programs are designed to address the needs of this wide audience, there is little hope that any level of schooling (elementary, middle, or high) will receive the attention it needs and deserves. Political pressure to offer alternative routes to administrative licensure is working its way into most state departments of education as well. The effects of this on the performance of middle level principals and the achievement of middle grades students have the potential to be devastating.

As a result of recent indictments against middle schools (see Bradley, 1998; Bradley & Manzo, 2000) and the heightened focus on school administrators, three major policy considerations have emerged: (1) strengthening the pre-service preparation of aspiring principals by improving certification requirements and formal academic work, (2) improving the process of selecting principals, and (3) improving and increasing the professional development opportunities for practicing middle level principals.

Summary and Overview

As middle level education moves into the 21st century new questions need to be asked and old ones revisited. Effective middle level principals are essential to current school reform initiatives. Their importance is heightened by the current indictments of the middle school movement (i.e., the return to K-8 school/grade configurations) and the general demand for accountability of schools. Emphasizing this renewed interest in the role of the principal, Olson (2000) wrote,

> After years of work on structural changes, standards and testing and ways of holding students accountable, the education policy world has turned its attention to the people charged with making the system work.... But nowhere is the focus on the human element in public education more prevalent than in the renewed recognition of the importance of strong and effective leadership. (p. 1)

For strong and effective leadership to become a reality, reflective practice and use of data related to one's performance are vital.

In this resource, we explore the following topics related to the leadership of middle level principals. In Part I we review the models of leadership that have dominated the field of educational administration and principal preparation programs, consider the position of developmentally responsive leadership in the larger body of school leadership literature, and present the theoretical foundations of our leadership model. A number of activities for both faculty and principal to engage in related to this examination of leadership are offered.

In Part II we present an instrument that is designed to measure the degree that a principal is developmentally responsive and explain the process of its development. We also present the results of a study that used this instrument and provide detailed instructions for scoring it should you choose to use it.

Part I
Leadership and the Middle School Principal

1. Models of School Leadership

Researchers in the field of educational administration have devoted considerable time and energy trying to understand school leadership. It is often noted that "leadership is one of the most widely talked about subjects and at the same time one of the most elusive and puzzling" (Cronin, 1993, p. 7). Echoing this belief, Chester Barnard (1948) wrote, "Leadership has been the subject of an extraordinary amount of dogmatically stated nonsense" (p. 80).

Leadership has been defined in myriad ways. It has been characterized as the creation and management of culture (Schein, 1985), the art of inducing others to do what one wants them to do (Bundel, 1959 as cited in Stogdill, 1974), and the dynamic force that stimulates, motivates, and coordinates an organization in the accomplishment of its objectives (Davis, 1942 as cited in Stogdill, 1974). Leaders perform certain functions that enlist the cooperation of members of an organization in performing duties associated with accomplishing the organization's mission. In schools, most of these functions are performed by the principal, but many are also carried out by others, such as team leaders.

According to Gardner (1990) the functions of leaders include

- Affirming values
- Setting goals
- Creating and sustaining trust
- Motivating
- Solving problems
- Representing the school or organization
- Managing.

Much has also been written that differentiates between management and leadership. In short, a good leader must posses the ability to do both. Table 2 contains some of the key words that have been associated with each of these areas of responsibility.

Table 2
The Difference Between a Manager and a Leader

MANAGER	LEADER
Administers	Innovates
Maintains	Develops
Relies on control	Inspires trust
Short-range view	Long-range perspective
Asks how and when	Asks why and what
Accepts the status-quo	Challenges the status-quo
Communicates directions	Communicates values
Seeks order/control	Encourages risk taking and innovation
Reactive	Active/Proactive
Rational	Emotional

Leadership builds a meaningful relationship between leaders and followers. The quality of that relationship and the resulting individual and organizational benefits are determined by one's orientation.

Out of the large body of research on leadership comes a variety of distinctly different models or approaches to leadership. Specifically, the following seven models have dominated contemporary writing about school leadership.

- Instructional leadership
- Transformational leadership
- Cultural leadership
- Moral leadership
- Participative leadership
- Managerial leadership
- Contingent leadership

Each of these seven models is distinct in its basic focus and the key assumptions on which it is based. There are, of course, many aspects of these models that are quite similar. For example, while instructional leadership targets issues related to curriculum and instruction, it also recognizes the importance of developing a positive school culture (cultural leadership).

We briefly examine each of these seven models in an attempt to build a foundation upon which to introduce the leadership model proposed in this book—developmentally responsive leadership. Essential references for further in-depth study for those interested.

Seven Leadership Models

1. Instructional leadership

As empirical evidence accumulated on the importance of principals' contributions to school improvement and student learning, researchers began to examine the characteristics of principals and their schools with special interest in the differences between high student achievement schools and low student achievement schools.

According to Smith and Andrews (1989), the principal who displays strong instructional leadership

- Places priority on curriculum and instructional issues
- Is dedicated to the goals of the school and the school district
- Is able to rally and mobilize resources to accomplish the school and district goals
- Creates a climate of high expectations in the school
- Functions as a leader with direct involvement in instructional policy by communicating with teachers, supporting and participating in staff development, establishing teacher incentives for the use of new instructional strategies, and displaying knowledge of curriculum materials
- Continuously monitors student progress and teacher effectiveness
- Demonstrates commitment to academic goals
- Effectively consults with others by involving faculty and other stakeholders in school decision making
- Recognizes time as a scarce resource and creates order and discipline by minimizing factors that may disrupt the learning process. (excerpted from pp. 8-9)

Duke (1987) identified five areas of work activity for instructional leaders that affect student learning and school outcomes: (1) teacher supervision and development, (2) teacher evaluation, (3) instructional management and support, (4) resource management, and (5) quality control. To underscore the belief that specific lists do not necessarily produce authentic instructional leaders, Duke provided a diagnostic checklist that includes a series of questions in each of the five areas (see pp. 297-299).

In Hallinger and Murphy's (1985) work, three broad categories of leadership practice define instructional leadership. These categories include: defining the school mission, managing the instructional program, and promoting school culture. Associated with these three broad categories are 21 specific practices, such as supervision of instruction. Considerable empirical evidence has accumulated in support of these leadership practices and their positive effects on student achievement.

2. Transformational leadership

A style of leadership receiving considerable attention today is transformational leadership. Burns (1978) proposed "transactional" and "transformational" leadership. Transactional leadership focuses on basic and largely extrinsic motives and needs and offers incentives such as monetary rewards, recognition, and promotions to secure workers' compliance with the leader's expectations and to persuade followers to work for the attainment of goals that are considered important to the organization (Foster, 1986). Transformational leadership is described as a process within which "leaders and followers raise one another to higher levels of morality and motivation" (Burns, p. 20). Transformational leaders may use rewards, but their purpose in doing so is to change workers' values and attitudes so that they internalize the goals, beliefs, and values that are essential for organizational effectiveness. They encourage members to commit to a vision of the future and seek to improve the problem-solving capacities of organizational members by building and strengthening member commitment to organization norms, values, and goals.

> Transformational leaders may use rewards, but their purpose in doing so is to change workers' values and attitudes so that they internalize the goals, beliefs, and values that are essential for organizational effectiveness.

This description highlights the concern for higher-order psychological needs for esteem, autonomy, and self-actualization as well as the moral issues of goodness, righteousness, duty, and obligation. The main focus of transformational leadership is on the commitments and capacities of organizational members. Higher levels of personal commitment to organizational goals and greater capacities for accomplishing those goals are assumed to result in extra effort and greater productivity.

Although the idea of transformational leadership was proposed by Burns (1978), Leithwood (1992; 1999) and his colleagues (Leithwood, Steinbach, & Raun, 1993) have added significantly to our understanding of this leadership model. Leithwood's model (1994) conceptualizes transformational leadership along seven dimensions: building school vision, establishing school goals, providing intellectual stimulation, offering individualized support, modeling best practices and organizational values, demonstrating high performance expectations, creating a productive school culture, and developing structures that foster participation in school decisions.

3. Cultural leadership

Numerous scholars have written about "cultural leadership," including Bennis (1983), Schein (1985), Deal and Kennedy (1982), Sarason (1996), and Sashkin and Walberg (1993). Culture is often defined as "the way we do things around here." Schein (1985) suggested that the most important thing that leaders do is help shape effective culture in which people will complete their work. He contends that culture "influences the ways in which group members perceive, think, and feel about the world thereby serving to stabilize the world, give meaning to it, and thereby reduce the anxiety that would result if we did not know how to categorize and respond to the environment" (p. 312). In short, an effective and functional school culture steers people in a common direction, provides a set of norms that defines what people accomplish and how, and provides a source of meaning and significance for teachers, students, and administrators.

Deal and Kennedy (1982) suggest that culture gives meaning to work, providing an understanding of how the organization moves from values and outcomes to work performance and, finally, to actual results. Our culture is important because it shapes the different ways we recognize and react to events, gives meaning and purpose to our work, and unites people. The goal of leadership is to make something as ill-defined as culture work for leaders and for the improvement of education. New ideas and genuine improvement may be elusive, unless we address the culture that underlies the operation of the school.

> New ideas and genuine improvement may be elusive, unless we address the culture that underlies the operation of the school.

Cunningham and Gresso (1993) found the flowing cultural elements essential for effective school operation:

- Collegiality, trust, integrity, and sufficient time for open, free-flowing communication
- An explicit, mutually shared, concrete vision of the ideal school
- A climate of mutual support, growth, and innovation
- Decisions based on values, interest, and expertise
- Empowerment and encouragement of staff to experiment, innovate, and share successes
- Central administrative support of individual school efforts
- Constant monitoring and feedback of results
- Face-to-face involvement of appropriate stakeholders.

(excerpted from pp. 267-268)

These cultural elements help leaders to achieve the continuing educational excellence being called for in almost every segment of our society.

4. Moral leadership

The rational or bureaucratic model of leadership assumes that administration is a technical enterprise and that administrative actions are morally neutral in their effect. During the 1990s, the normative dimension of leadership has been one of the fastest growing areas of leadership study (see Duke, 1996). Those writing about moral leadership argue that values are a central part of all leadership and administrative practice (see Bates, 1993; Evers & Lakomski, 1991; Greenfield, 1991; Hodgkinson, 1991). Hodgkinson (1991) claimed, "values constitute the essential problem of leadership.... If there are no value conflicts then there is no need for leadership" (p. 11). Individuals whose actions affect others' lives and welfare are moral agents who should be guided in their actions by principle rather than by emotion, expediency, or the prospect of personal gain (Schrag, 1978).

According to Seyfarth (1999), school administrators operate from one of several ethical positions. They may be guided in their leadership actions (1) by personal preferences (inner beliefs about right and wrong), (2) by calculating the end results of contemplated actions, (3) by rules ethics (upholding laws, policies, and regulations), (4) by consensual norms (expressed values of the work group), or (5) by public opinion (i.e., parental and community views). In short, the focus of moral leadership is on the values and ethics of the leader, so authority and influence are to be derived from what is perceived to be right and good.

Barnard (1938) spoke eloquently of the moral dimensions of leadership, calling attention to moral creativeness as the highest expression of responsibility (p. 261). The leader does not create anything of lasting value. That creation comes about through cooperation, and it is the work of the organization as a whole. The leader accomplishes this through the "creation of faith" by serving as a catalyst for human effort. "Cooperation, not leadership, is the creative process; but leadership is the indispensable fulminator of its forces" (p. 259).

5. Participative leadership

Participative leadership (i.e., group, shared, teacher leadership) stresses the decision-making processes of the group (see Hayes, 1995; Murphy & Hallinger, 1992). One argument for participative leadership sets forth the belief that participation will enhance organizational effectiveness. Another argument bases its case for participation on democratic principles. In this model, authority and influence are available to any legitimate stakeholder in the school, involving teachers and parents much more in school decision making.

> The prime example of participative leadership is the move to site-based management.

Citing changes such as increased complexity, uncertainty, ambiguity, workload, and expectations for school innovation, Murphy and Hallinger (1992) conclude that school leaders will need to adopt a more participatory form of leadership. This includes being more consultative, open, and democratic and involves teachers, parents, and other education stakeholders. From the list of restructuring or reform initiatives undertaken in the past 25 years, the prime example of participative leadership is the move to site-based management.

6. Managerial leadership

Managerial leadership focuses on the functions, tasks, and behaviors of the leader and assumes that if these functions are carried out competently, the work of others in the organization will be facilitated, resulting in an effectively functioning organization. Most approaches to managerial leadership assume that organizational members behave rationally (see Achilles, 1992; Bolman & Deal, 1991; Dunning, 1993). Authority and influence are allocated to formal positions in proportion to the status of those positions in the organization's hierarchy.

Managerial leaders focus on policy implementation, maintaining organizational stability, and ensuring that routine organizational tasks are "done right." Much attention is given to planning, organizing, supervising, coordinating, budgeting, and staffing. This emphasis is in stark contrast to leaders who make policy, work for organizational growth and development, and make sure the "right things get done" (Bennis & Nanus, 1985).

When managerial leadership is applied to the educational setting, Duke and Leithwood (1994) found the following ten tasks associated with managerial leadership.

1. Providing adequate financial and material resources
2. Distributing financial and material resources so that they are most useful
3. Anticipating predictable problems and developing effective and efficient means for responding to them
4. Managing the school faculty
5. Managing the student body
6. Maintaining effective communication patterns with staff, students, community members, and district office staff
7. Accommodating policies and initiatives undertaken by the district office in ways that assist with school improvement goals
8. Buffering staff so as to reduce disruptions to the instructional program
9. Mediating conflict and differences in expectations
10. Attending to the political demands of school functioning. (pp. 23-35)

7. Contingent leadership

This leadership model focuses on how leaders respond to the unique organizational circumstances or problems that arise (see Blake & Mouton, 1964; Hersey & Blanchard, 1977). A leader's effectiveness in a given situation depends upon the "fit" between his or her style and the task, authority level, and nature of the group. The interactions between these various combinations yield different results in different situations.

This model assumes that there are wide variations in the contexts for leadership and that to be effective, these contexts require different leadership responses. Also assumed in this model is the belief that those who hold leadership positions have the ability to master a large repertoire of leadership practices.

Fiedler's (1967) work is important to consider here. His model postulates that there is a situational nature to effective leader behavior. He concluded that the interaction of three factors determines leadership effectiveness.

> This model assumes that there are wide variations in the contexts for leadership and that to be effective, these contexts require different leadership responses.

1. Leader-Member Relations: This refers to the leader's feeling of being accepted by subordinates. A leader's authority depends, at least in part, on the acceptance of the group to be led. A person who is respected by and inspires loyalty in the work group needs few of the vestments of rank to get the group to perform the task at hand in a willing and competent manner.

2. Task Structure: This is the degree to which the subordinate's tasks are routine and precisely defined, as opposed to being relatively unstructured and loosely defined.

3. Power Position: This refers to the power inherent in the leadership position and includes the means available to the leader from those at higher administrative levels and authority. This is the extent to which the leader possesses reward, coercive, and legitimate power.

In measuring the style of the leader, Fiedler used two points of measurement: task orientation and relationship orientation. Fiedler hypothesized that group productivity resulted from a match between the leader's orientation (task or relationship orientation) and the favorableness of the particular work context (a mix of personal traits, group beliefs, situational variables).

Summary

In sum, these approaches to conceptualizing school leadership offer eclectic and overlapping perspectives on what should be the focus of the principal's attention and how leadership manifests itself in practice. We hold that while considering the context in which school leadership occurs, the developmental characteristics of the students have been either ignored or forgotten as a basis for a model of leadership.

FOLLOW-UP ACTIVITIES

Faculty and Staff

- Provide your school's faculty and staff with the names and descriptions of the seven leadership models. Form small groups to discuss each of these models. Ask each group to identify the characteristics and behaviors of principals and/or school leaders (i.e., teacher leaders) who exemplify each model. Finish this activity by facilitating a large-group discussion of the small-group responses.

- Have the faculty and staff create a list of the qualities and characteristics they would want to see exhibited by a middle level principal. Ask that faculty and staff agree (i.e., a majority vote or consensus) on each item before adding it to the master list of characteristics. How do these qualities fit in the seven leadership models presented in this section of the book? Which quality does the faculty and staff consider to be most critical? Why?

- Engage your faculty and staff in a discussion of the terms *developmentally appropriate* and *developmentally responsive*. What do these terms mean? How has each term been defined in relation to middle level teachers? How do the terms apply to the middle level principal?

- Have a discussion focused on the question: Have changing conditions (i.e., No Child Left Behind, economic conditions, others) resulted in a change in leadership style at your school? What has changed? Why?

Principal

- Reflect on your leadership style as principal of a middle school. Which of the seven leadership models best characterizes you?

- List specific actions you take as a middle school principal to support your choice of the model that best describes your leadership style.

- Reflect on your experiences in schools prior to serving as principal. Under what type of leadership did you respond most positively and productively? What type of leadership caused you to resist the leader? What does this tell you about your leadership style?

- Has your leadership style evolved over time? On what larger ideas (i.e., philosophy) is your leadership style based?

2. The Developmentally Responsive Middle Level Principal

In addition to these seven models of school leadership, we put forth an eighth—*developmentally responsive leadership*. Developmentally responsive leadership is grounded in the belief that schools should be organized and operated around the developmental characteristics of the students they educate.

We propose a three-dimensional model for the developmentally responsive middle school principal. The features of this model include: (1) responsiveness to the developmental needs of middle grades students, (2) responsiveness to the developmental needs of the faculty who support learning for middle grades students, and (3) responsiveness to the development of the middle school itself as a unique innovating entity. This perspective is supported by several theoretical foci. First, recent theoretical writing on the "distributed perspective" (Spillane, Halverson, & Diamond, 2001) describes the unit of analysis for the study of schools as "leadership practice in a school unit" (p. 24), rather than the leader acting in isolation. From a distributive perspective, "leadership practice (both thinking and activity) emerges in and through the interaction of leaders, followers, and the situation" (p. 27). This means viewing leadership as a principal's interaction with faculty, students, the distinctive nature of the middle school itself, and other key stakeholders. This necessitates connecting with students, their needs, and their current developmental circumstances.

The perspective that a leader's work needs to be seen in a "distributive" way does not necessarily lead to a developmentally responsive approach, although it does clear the path for such a disposition. How will middle level principals frame their school context? Sergiovanni's (1996) use of Tonnies' (1957) *gemeinschaft* (community/moral) and *gesselschaft* (society/formal) as a continuum now becomes relevant.

While we do not support placing the middle school leader at the extreme of *gemeinschaft* (that is the head of a purely community enterprise), we do believe that leadership at this level of education belongs closer to that end of the continuum and less to the extreme of gesselschaft or social/formal organization. Our reason is that we are speaking about young people entering adolescence. This is a particularly stressful and momentous developmental period with specific cognitive distinctions (Piaget, 1952), and social/emotional challenges (Erikson, 1964). Working with young adolescents requires a strong orientation toward the ethic of care (Beck, 1994; Noddings, 1992) as its underpinning. This does not exclude challenging academic standards, nor

> Developmentally responsive middle level leaders are in the best position to help learners at this stage because they will deal with students as they are at a time when recognition of their social, emotional and intellectual needs is remarkably acute.

does it preclude middle grades learners from interacting with the demands of the adult world (gesselschaft). We hold that developmentally responsive middle level leaders are in the best position to help learners at this stage because they will deal with students when recognition of their social, emotional, and intellectual needs is remarkably acute. Developmentally responsive leaders will understand the needs of their students and use this knowledge with teachers, staff, and families to understand middle grades learners' zone of proximal development or ZPD (Vygotsky, 1978). Effective scaffolds coming from this analysis are based upon understanding and responding to middle grades learners' needs.

We believe that this kind of leadership, especially at the middle level, holds the best chance for students to identify with the school (Finn, 1989; Leithwood & Jantzi, 1999) and thus be engaged with the school's learning agenda. In the three-dimensional model proposed, the developmentally responsive middle level principal is responsive to the needs of students, faculty, and the school itself.

Responsiveness to the Developmental Needs of Young Adolescents

Regarding curriculum, instruction, and assessment. There is an urgency to see the clash of middle level social/community needs and academic achievement in a new light—first, to acknowledge and understand the nature of the conflict and second, to be well grounded not only in relevant curriculum, instruction, and assessment but the related developmental issues of middle grades learners (see NMSA, 2003, pp. 19-23). The energy arising from this tension can be used to enhance both quality time to work out the social/emotional needs of this age group and to delve more deeply into significant content (i.e., acting out a historic drama).

In this way, the learner in the middle grades is not merely "in-between" (a definition of what they are not, neither elementary nor high school—therefore, a weak definition), but a special kind of learner with unique gifts that are short lived (since no one stays a middle grades student for very long) and, therefore, all the more precious. The developmentally responsive principal will think about curriculum-instruction-assessment and will be able to share that vision with the faculty and stakeholders and develop concrete plans with them. Developmentally appropriate practice requires that both teachers and principals integrate what they know about young adolescent development and the implications of this knowledge for how and when to teach the content of the curriculum and how to assess what students have learned.

Regarding school culture and the commitment to community versus bureaucracy. While we find Sergiovanni's (1996) use of community attractive, especially as a metaphor for middle grades leadership, we do not consider middle schools to be simple, easily understood communities. Extending Sergiovanni's metaphor of community, Enomoto (1997) added the notion of nested communities; that is, co-existent spheres within a school or "multiple, overlapping and nested cultures" (p. 529). The developmentally responsive principal must understand and work with these nested communities. Developmentally appropriate practices occur within a context that supports the development of relationships between adults and students, among students, and between teachers and families.

Regarding responsiveness to the at-risk behaviors unique to middle grades learners. The developmentally responsive middle level principal will understand and help faculty, staff, and families design effective programs relevant to the specific potential at-risk behaviors of students at this age (Carnegie Council on Adolescent Development, 1989; Eccles & Midgley, 1989). Developmental trajectories diverge in young adolescence toward either healthy adjustment or psychopathology (Petersen & Hamburg, 1986). Declines in academic motivation, perceived competence, intrinsic interest in school (Harter, 1981), and self-esteem (Eccles, Midgley, & Adler, 1984) are common, not to mention anxiety, depression, substance abuse, and antisocial behaviors (see Hankin, Abramson, Silva, McGee, Moffitt, & Angell, 1998).

Regarding relationships with families in transition from parenting children in elementary school to parenting teenagers. The developmentally responsive leader assists parents in understanding their children at this unique stage of their lives. They help in preparing for the physical, emotional, and social changes as well as in understanding the stresses that may lead to at-risk behavior. Moreover, there is a need to engage families and the wider community in understanding the developmental nature of the family itself so that parents can more effectively interact with their middle grades children. These will likely involve new behaviors and require parents to be increasingly comfortable with ambiguity (being pushed away by the child and yet still needing to show approval, for instance).

This means that the developmentally responsive middle school principal must understand that there is a developmental cycle in families. They must also understand where particular families may be in their life cycle as well as the developmental qualities of parents of middle grades students. Finally, this means understanding how adult learners (parents, faculty and board members) engage new ideas.

Responsiveness to the Needs of Faculty

We believe that middle schools require a particular kind of teacher—one who is attracted to the energy and complexity of young adolescents and combines empathy with skills in modeling effective strategies for students of this age. Knowledge of the developmental circumstances of middle grades learners matched with an affinity to curriculum content that is rich, demanding, and highly interactive is also important. A commitment to the middle school's instructional and community-building structures listed above is a high priority as well, especially teaming. The role of the developmentally responsive principal is to value these educators and to be highly demanding when the opportunity presents itself to hire and assign new faculty. This also means leadership advocacy for the kind of instruction and organization that will create community.

Finally, developmentally responsive leaders need to make a careful study of the career cycle of successful middle grades teachers and apply the lessons of that study to their setting.

Responsiveness to the Needs of the School

Moving outward from the students' developmental needs in point one above and the teachers' needs in point two, the developmentally responsive middle school leader must see the continued growth of the school itself as an ongoing issue. This means understanding the cycle of school innovation (Gross, 1998) as well as the politics of districts and state governance issues. It also means understanding the unique structures that have been identified for effective middle level education, such as advisory programs, transition programs, interdisciplinary curriculum, and exploratory programs. In this way, leaders are best able to nurture, protect, and defend the hard work that they helped to initiate and to work toward the school's ultimate goal of improved student achievement and socioemotional development.

The literature regarding middle level education and middle school reform is replete with references to "developmental appropriateness" and "developmentally responsive" schools, curricula, practices, structures, and strategies. Pivotal to this discussion, but conspicuously absent, is the role of middle level leadership in implementing such reform efforts.

Developmentally responsive leadership results from the process of making decisions about the well being and education of children, about faculty, and about the school itself, based on the following kinds of information:

1. What is known about human development and learning—knowledge of age-related characteristics that permit general predictions within an age range about what activities, materials, interactions, or experiences will be safe, healthy, interesting, achievable, and challenging to young adolescents

2. What is known about the strengths, interests, and needs of each individual student to be able to adapt for and be responsive to inevitable individual differences

3. Knowledge of the social and cultural contexts in which children live to ensure that learning experiences are meaningful, relevant, and respectful for the participating children and their families.
        (National Association for the Education of Young Children, 1997)

Based both on extensive research (see Brown & Anfara, 2002; Brown, Anfara, & Gross, 2002) and feedback from middle level principals, we define the *developmentally responsive middle level principal* as one who is

1. Responsive to the needs of students:
    *   understands the intellectual, physical, psychological, social, and moral/ethical characteristics of young adolescents
    *   establishes a learning environment that reflects the needs of young adolescents

- purposely designs programs, policies, curriculum, and procedures that reflect the characteristics of young adolescents
- believes that all students can succeed
- views parents and the community as partners, not adversaries
- provides students with opportunities to explore a rich variety of topics to develop their identity and demonstrate their competence
- provides students with opportunities to explore, make mistakes, and grow in a safe, caring environment.

2. Responsive to the needs of faculty:
   - understands the necessity of reconnecting educational administration to the processes of teaching and learning
   - emotionally invested in the job
   - shares a vision for continuous organizational improvement and growth
   - creates opportunities for faculty professional development that address strategies for meeting the needs of young adolescents
   - encourages teachers to employ a wide variety of instructional and assessment approaches and materials
   - provides teachers with the resources necessary to effectively perform their teaching responsibilities.

3. Responsive to needs of the school:
   - knowledgeable about and can implement the components of the middle school concept
   - acts as a responsible catalyst for change and understands that change requires time, training, trust, and tangible support
   - flexible and able to deal with ambiguity and chaos
   - advocates for middle level education and what is best for young adolescents.

> Developmentally responsive middle level leadership recognizes and embraces learners' developmental levels as providing the basis for all school curricular and instructional practices.

If middle level reform is going to achieve the goal of a positive educational environment that ensures student cognitive and affective development, middle level principals must come to a more complete understanding of their role in this process. They must acknowledge that different skills and knowledge are necessary for leadership at this level. Being truly "responsive" entails a readiness and willingness to react to suggestions, influences, and appeals and to reply appropriately and sympathetically. It requires "responding to current challenges, engaging in thoughtful and reflective discussions, and actively and openly embracing the revision and refinement of programs" (Williamson & Johnston, 1999, p. 11). Developmentally responsive middle level leadership recognizes and embraces learners' developmental levels as providing the basis for all school curricular and instructional practices, as well as the overall teaching-learning environment (Manning, 1993).

FOLLOW-UP ACTIVITIES

Faculty and Staff

- Lead a brainstorming session in which faculty and staff list all of the possible ways that a principal can demonstrate: (a) responsiveness to young adolescents, (b) responsiveness to faculty, and (c) responsiveness to the needs of the school.

- Review the developmental characteristics of young adolescents. Look at the following five areas: intellectual, emotional/psychological, physical, moral/ethical, and social. To illustrate these developmental characteristics, ask faculty and staff to think about actual students (without mentioning names) when providing examples of these developmental characteristics.

- As part of faculty and staff professional development read Nel Noddings' (2002) *Educating Moral People: A Caring Alternative to Character Education,* available through Teachers College Press. Have groups of faculty present the chapters as part of monthly faculty meetings.

- Have faculty and staff generate a list of all of the varied instructional and assessment strategies used by teachers in your school. Which would be developmentally appropriate for young adolescents? Why? Which are not? Why not?

- Identify the at-risk behaviors that students in your school have displayed. Which at-risk behavior ranks highest on this list? Identify programs that have been created and/or implemented to address these at-risk student behaviors.

- What activities or programs does your school use to assist parents in understanding young adolescents and this unique developmental stage? Are these programs meeting the needs of parents? Brainstorm additional activities that your school could provide for parents.

- Identify the qualities and characteristics of effective middle level teachers in open brainstorming. From these qualities and characteristics have a small committee consolidate and create a checklist of characteristics that teachers and staff can use in assessing their individual effectiveness.

- Role-play the hiring of a middle level teacher at a faculty meeting. Create the scenario and have someone act as principal and another person portray the teacher. Critique the performance. Were the questions asked ones that would reveal the candidate's understanding of the middle school concept?

Principal

- How do new conditions, such as the No Child Left Behind Act, support or conflict with your ability to be a developmentally responsive leader?

- Identify allies at the district level who can support your efforts in being a developmentally responsive leader.

- Recall the specific things you have done to promote relationships between students and students, faculty and students, and the school and its parents and immediate community. Make a list of these items and brainstorm other possible actions that would contribute to a heightened sense of school community.

- Read anew the section of *This We Believe: Successful Schools for Young Adolescents* (NMSA, 2003) that focuses on courageous and collaborative leadership (see pages 10-11). Reflect on these ideas in relation to your practice.

- Reflect on your educational administration preparation program and recent professional development activities. Did either or both contribute significantly to the skills, knowledge, and dispositions that you need to effectively lead a middle school? If so, how? If not, where and how did you obtain the skills and knowledge that help you succeed as a middle level principal?

- Add to your professional library for later study and reference *From the Desk of the Middle School Principal: Leadership Responsive to the Needs of Young Adolescents* (Brown & Anfara, 2002), available from Scarecrow Press, and Lynn Beck's (1994) *Reclaiming Educational Administration as a Caring Profession,* available through Teachers College Press.

Part II

Determining One's Status as a
Developmentally Responsive Middle Level Principal

3. The Middle Level Leadership Questionnaire

The Middle Level Leadership Questionnaire (MLLQ) focuses on the actions (behaviors) of middle level principals in areas related to students, teachers, parents, the curriculum, professional development, school-community relations, and the structuring of the school day. This instrument was originally developed from research findings on 98 middle school principals (Brown & Anfara, 2002).

The MLLQ consists of three sections: (1) demographic characteristics of the participants, (2) behaviors of middle school principals, and (3) an inventory of middle school practices. The instrument is designed to evaluate behaviors of middle school principals, with the demographic and middle school practices portions being ancillary. Initially, a 65-item Likert scale using a five-point response format (5=frequently, if not always; 4=fairly often; 3=sometimes; 2=once in a while; 1=not at all) was created to measure the behaviors of middle school principals. Positive and negative statements were included to address response bias; 14 of the 65 items were negatively worded statements. The MLLQ presented in this chapter contains 33 Likert items. Detailed information on how validity and reliability were achieved is provided in Appendix A.

A careful study of the instrument included here would be of value to a principal seeking to better understand developmentally responsive administration; however, it needs to be completed by a principal as thoughtfully and honestly as possible. The results provide a measure of the degree to which a principal views himself or herself as developmentally responsive. Scoring methods and standards for comparison were developed in a pilot study involving 9 principals and 251 teachers and are detailed in Chapter 4.

The principal should complete the instrument in one sitting having selected a quiet place and adequate time for so doing. Administering the teachers' form of the instrument to the faculty should be done only after the faculty has been adequately prepared and when the principal feels comfortable with taking this step. A degree of readiness needs to exist and usually is preceded by ample discussion on leadership as suggested in Chapter 1; and a teacher-principal relationship that will both free teachers to make their best professional judgments and ensure that the principal is secure enough to accept these judgments. Anonymity should be ensured by having the unsigned, completed questionnaires returned in sealed envelopes and placed in a collection box. A very small committee may be charged with scoring the questionnaires.

MIDDLE LEVEL LEADERSHIP QUESTIONNAIRE
Principal's Form

The Middle Level Leadership Questionnaire (MLLQ) focuses on the actions (behaviors) of middle level principals (typically grades 6-8) in areas related to students, teachers, parents, the curriculum, professional development, school-community relations, and the structuring of the school day. You are asked to reflect on your actions as a middle school principal.

PART ONE. Demographic Information

Directions: *Please complete the following background information before completing the questionnaire.*

Name (optional): _____

School: _____

Age (circle one):   20-24   25-35   36-46   47-57   58+

Gender (circle one):   M   F

Race: American Indian or Alaskan Eskimo_____   Hispanic_____
       Asian or Pacific Islander_____   White_____
       Black_____   Other_____

Level of education:_____

Years of teaching before becoming a principal: _____

Principal certification (circle one):

   elementary   middle   K-12   secondary   other

Years as a principal:_____

Years as principal at this school: _____

Please include any personal or professional information you feel would be important for the researchers to know.

_____
_____
_____
_____
_____
_____

PART TWO. Questionnaire (Principal's Form)

Directions: Listed below are statements that describe a variety of behaviors middle school principals may exhibit. Reflecting on your behaviors as a middle school principal please respond to each item by filling in the circle to mark the appropriate response following each statement.

5	4	3	2	1
Frequently, if not always	Fairly often	Sometimes	Once in a while	Not at all

As the principal of a middle school, I ...

	5	4	3	2	1
1. design and implement policies and procedures that reflect the needs of young adolescents.	O	O	O	O	O
2. promote the development of caring relationships between teachers, staff, and students through structures like advisory periods, etc.	O	O	O	O	O
3. provide transition programs from middle to high school for my middle school students.	O	O	O	O	O
4. provide transition programs from elementary to middle school for my middle school students.	O	O	O	O	O
5. organize the curriculum around real-life concepts.	O	O	O	O	O
6. advocate for middle schools and the middle school concept in the school district.	O	O	O	O	O
7. prepare a daily schedule that includes time for team planning and meeting.	O	O	O	O	O
8. stay current on what the research says about best practices for middle schools.	O	O	O	O	O

9. group students and teachers in small learning communities.	○	○	○	○	○
10. have a vision of what an exemplary middle school is and strive to bring that vision to life.	○	○	○	○	○
11. provide curricular materials that enhance young adolescents' acceptance of self and others and that enable them to accept differences and similarities among people.	○	○	○	○	○
12. provide adequate counseling/advisory opportunities.	○	○	○	○	○
13. demonstrate an understanding of the intellectual, physical, psychological, and social characteristics of young adolescents.	○	○	○	○	○
14. demonstrate an understanding of the relationship between the cognitive and affective needs of young adolescents.	○	○	○	○	○
15. spend time each day with students.	○	○	○	○	○
16. provide students with opportunities to explore a rich variety of topics in order to develop their identity and demonstrate their competence.	○	○	○	○	○
17. develop connections with and involve families in the education of their children.	○	○	○	○	○
18. provide age-appropriate, co-curricular (or extra-curricular) activities.	○	○	○	○	○

19. provide students with opportunities to explore, make mistakes, and grow in a safe, caring environment.	○	○	○	○	○
20. encourage mature value systems by providing opportunities for students to examine options of behavior and to study consequences of various actions.	○	○	○	○	○
21. regard young adolescents as resources in planning and program development and involve them in meaningful roles.	○	○	○	○	○
22. make decisions based on young adolescent development and effective middle level practices.	○	○	○	○	○
23. allow teachers and students to plan activities that integrate genders.	○	○	○	○	○
24. provide time for general education teachers to collaborate with special education teachers in order to meet the diverse needs of young adolescents.	○	○	○	○	○
25. encourage teachers to modify time, grouping, and instructional strategies to help individual students achieve mastery of subject matter.	○	○	○	○	○
26. encourage teachers in their efforts to respond to the needs of young adolescents.	○	○	○	○	○
27. encourage teachers in their use of a wide variety of instructional approaches and materials.	○	○	○	○	○
28. encourage active discovery learning on the part of students rather than teacher lecture.	○	○	○	○	○

29. encourage activities such as special interest classes and hands-on learning.	○	○	○	○	○
30. create opportunities for professional development of teachers/staff that address strategies for meeting the needs of young adolescents.	○	○	○	○	○
31. support appropriate instructional strategies with the necessary resources (i.e., money, time needed, etc.).	○	○	○	○	○
32. encourage teachers to make connections across disciplines to reinforce important concepts.	○	○	○	○	○
33. require teachers to provide classroom activities that address the needs of academically diverse learners who vary greatly in readiness, interest, and learning profile.	○	○	○	○	○

PART THREE. Inventory of Middle School Practices

Directions: Please put a check in front of each of the middle school components that are implemented in your school to an extent that you would invite others to observe them in action.

_____ Exploratory curriculum   _____ Teaming

_____ Varied teaching and learning approaches   _____ Advisory programs

_____ Flexible scheduling   _____ Involvement of families
                                                              and communities

_____ Democratic governance of the school (with teachers, parents, community members)

_____ Programs that promote good health, wellness, and safety

MIDDLE LEVEL LEADERSHIP QUESTIONNAIRE
Teacher's Form

The Middle Level Leadership Questionnaire (MLLQ) focuses on the actions (behaviors) of middle level principals (typically grades 6-8) in areas related to students, teachers, parents, the curriculum, professional development, school-community relations, and the structuring of the school day. You are asked to reflect on the actions of your middle school principal.

PART ONE. Demographic Information

Directions: Please complete the following background information before completing the questionnaire.

Name (optional): _____

School: _____

Age (circle one):   20-24   25-35   36-46   47-57   58+

Gender (circle one):   M   F

Race: American Indian or Alaskan Eskimo_____   Hispanic_____
         Asian or Pacific Islander_____   White_____
         Black_____   Other_____

Level of education:_____

Years of teaching: _____

Certification (circle one):

   elementary   middle   K-12   secondary   other

Subjects certified to teach:_____

Please include any personal or professional information you feel would be important for the researchers to know.

_____
_____
_____
_____
_____
_____

PART TWO. Questionnaire (Teacher's Form)

Directions: Listed below are statements that describe a variety of behaviors middle school principals may exhibit. Reflecting on your principal's behaviors, please respond to each item by filling in the appropriate response following each statement.

5	4	3	2	1
Frequently, if not always	Fairly often	Sometimes	Once in a while	Not at all

The principal of my middle school ...

	5	4	3	2	1
1. designs and implements policies and procedures that reflect the needs of young adolescents.	O	O	O	O	O
2. promotes the development of caring relationships between teachers, staff, and students through structures like advisory periods, etc.	O	O	O	O	O
3. provides transition programs from middle to high school for my middle school students.	O	O	O	O	O
4. provides transition programs from elementary to middle school for my middle school students.	O	O	O	O	O
5. organizes the curriculum around real-life concepts.	O	O	O	O	O
6. advocates for middle schools and the middle school concept in the school district.	O	O	O	O	O
7. prepares a daily schedule that includes time for team planning and meeting.	O	O	O	O	O
8. stays current on what the research says about best practices for middle schools.	O	O	O	O	O

9. groups students and teachers in small learning communities.	O	O	O	O	O
10. has a vision of what an exemplary middle school is and strives to bring that vision to life.	O	O	O	O	O
11. provides curricular materials that enhance young adolescents' acceptance of self and others and that enable them to accept differences and similarities among people.	O	O	O	O	O
12. provides adequate counseling/advisory opportunities.	O	O	O	O	O
13. demonstrates an understanding of the intellectual, physical, psychological, and social characteristics of young adolescents.	O	O	O	O	O
14. demonstrates an understanding of the relationship between the cognitive and affective needs of young adolescents.	O	O	O	O	O
15. spends time each day with students.	O	O	O	O	O
16. provides students with opportunities to explore a rich variety of topics in order to develop their identity and demonstrate their competence.	O	O	O	O	O
17. develops connections with and involves families in the education of their children.	O	O	O	O	O
18. provides age-appropriate, co-curricular (or extra-curricular) activities.	O	O	O	O	O

19. provides students with opportunities to explore, make mistakes, and grow in a safe, caring environment.	O	O	O	O	O
20. encourages mature value systems by providing opportunities for students to examine options of behavior and to study consequences of various actions.	O	O	O	O	O
21. regards young adolescents as resources in planning and program development and involves them in meaningful roles.	O	O	O	O	O
22. makes decisions based on young adolescent development and effective middle level practices.	O	O	O	O	O
23. allows teachers and students to plan activities that integrate genders.	O	O	O	O	O
24. provides time for general education teachers to collaborate with special education teachers in order to meet the diverse needs of young adolescents.	O	O	O	O	O
25. encourages teachers to modify time, grouping, and instructional strategies to help individual students achieve mastery of subject matter.	O	O	O	O	O
26. encourages teachers in their efforts to respond to the needs of young adolescents.	O	O	O	O	O
27. encourages teachers in their use of a wide variety of instructional approaches and materials.	O	O	O	O	O
28. encourages active discovery learning on the part of students rather than teacher lecture.	O	O	O	O	O

29. encourages activities such as special interest classes and hands-on learning.	○	○	○	○	○
30. creates opportunities for professional development of teachers/staff that address strategies for meeting the needs of young adolescents.	○	○	○	○	○
31. supports appropriate instructional strategies with the necessary resources (i.e., money, time needed, etc.).	○	○	○	○	○
32. encourages teachers to make connections across disciplines to reinforce important concepts.	○	○	○	○	○
33. requires teachers to provide classroom activities that address the needs of academically diverse learners who vary greatly in readiness, interest, and learning profile.	○	○	○	○	○

PART THREE. Inventory of Middle School Practices

Directions: Please put a check in front of each of the middle school components that are implemented in your school to an extent that you would invite others to observe them in action.

_____ Exploratory curriculum   _____ Teaming

_____ Varied teaching and learning approaches   _____ Advisory programs

_____ Flexible scheduling   _____ Involvement of families
                                                                                    and communities

_____ Democratic governance of the school (with teachers, parents, community members)

_____ Programs that promote good health, wellness, and safety

4. Scoring and Interpreting the Results

Provided below are steps to score the instruments once administered within a school. You will be directed how to compare your scores with your teachers' scores and the scores from the normative sample used in the creation of the MLLQ. Please note that the scores in this study are based on a sample of 260 participants within 9 schools, and there is not a normal distribution of means (i.e., mean scores are negatively skewed).

Step 1:   Score each item for each respondent (teachers) with the appropriate Likert number (1, 2, 3, 4, or 5). (There are no negatively worded items, so there is no need to worry about reverse scoring.)

Step 2:   Calculate an average (mean) score for each of the 33 items on the MLLQ. (Remember to add all of your teachers' responses for each item together and then divide by the total number of teacher responses.)

Step 3:   Sum the average (mean) scores of the items associated with each factor (see Appendix B for a description of each factor):

Factor One
     Sum means of questions 11, 12, 13, 17, 18, 19, 23, 26, 28, 29, 30, 31, 32, 33
Factor Two
     Sum means of questions 1, 2, 4, 6, 8, 10, 27
Factor Three
     Sum means of questions 7, 9, 14, 20, 22
Factor Four
     Sum means of questions 5, 15, 16, 21
Factor Five
     Sum means of questions 3, 24, 25

Step 4: Divide each sum above by the number of questions within a given factor (e.g., Factor One has 14 questions, so an example may look like 65/14 = 4.64). This gives you the total mean scores for your teachers for each of the five factors. These five scores represent your level of developmental responsiveness on each of the five factors.

Step 5: Record your (the principal's) scores for each of the 33 items. Calculate the total mean scores for each of the five factors as you did for your teachers.

Step 6: You may now compare your teachers' mean scores for each factor with the mean scores of teachers in the normative sample in Table 4 (see Topic 4 for this table). Table 4 also allows you to compare your scores to those of other middle school principals in the normative sample.

Step 7: Compare your scores to those of your teachers. (Note: Principals tend to rate themselves more highly than do their teachers.)

Step 8: Compare your total mean scores for each factor in Table 3 to determine the percentile of your school's factor scores against the factor scores from the normative sample. For example, a mean score of 4.44 for Factor One, would indicate that your school's responses fell within the 60th percentile when compared to the nine schools' responses in the sample used to develop the MLLQ.

Table 3

Percentile Scores

Mean Scores	Factor One	Factor Two	Factor Three	Factor Four	Factor Five
2.0 - 2.5	2%	2%	2%	7%	3.5%
2.51- 3.0	5%	7%	5%	22%	17%
3.01 - 3.5	15%	10%	10%	45%	30%
3.51 - 4.0	30%	20%	30%	67%	45%
4.01 - 4.5	60%	45%	55%	85%	70%
4.51 - 5.0	Above 60%	Above 45%	Above 55%	Above 85%	Above 70%

Computing the Standardized Scores for the Five MLLQ Factors

To convert your school's mean scores to standardized scores with a mean of 500 and a standard deviation of 100, use the following SdS (Standardized Score) formulas:

SdS for Factor One = 100(Factor One Total Mean Score − 4.26) / .607 + 500

First compute the difference between your total mean school score on Factor One and the total mean for the normative sample (Factor One Total Mean Score − 4.26). Then multiply the difference by 100 [100(Factor One Total Mean Score − 4.26)]. Next divide the product by the standard deviation of the normative sample (.607). Then add 500 to the result. You have computed a standardized score (SdS) for your school's Factor One (i.e., factor for Developmentally Appropriate Learning Environment/Support of Teachers).

Repeat the process for each factor as follows:

SdS for Factor Two = 100(Factor Two Total Mean Score − 4.42) / .678 + 500
SdS for Factor Three = 100(Factor Three Total Mean Score − 4.32) / .678 + 500
SdS for Factor Four = 100(Factor Four Total Mean Score − 3.73) / .763 + 500
SdS for Factor Five = 100(Factor Five Total Mean Score − 4.07) / .849 + 500

Check your school's standardized scores against the normative data for the five factors documented in Table 4. This table represents approximate standardized scores in terms of standard deviations (SD) from the mean score of the normative sample. Hence, 99% is three SDs above/below average, 97% is two SD's above or below average, and 84% is one SD above or below average.

Table 4

Standardized Scoring Table for the Five MLLQ Factors

If the score is:					
Factor One	Factor Two	Factor Three	Factor Four	Factor Five	Standard Deviation Rating
165	160	135	235	200	it is lower than 99% of the schools
260	215	230	310	250	it is lower than 97% of the schools
370	400	380	375	355	it is lower than 84% of the schools
510	**520**	**500**	**485**	**510**	**it is average**
590	565	575	585	585	it is higher than 84% of the schools
615	575	600	655	600	it is higher than 97% of the schools
620	580	605	665	605	it is higher than 99% of the schools

Computing an Overall MLLQ Standardized Index Score

Once you have computed the standardized scores for the five factors in the MLLQ, then you can calculate an overall index score. The overall index of your school's developmentally responsive leadership can be computed as follows:

$$\frac{(SdS\ for\ Factor\ One)+(SdS\ for\ Factor\ Two)+(SdS\ for\ Factor\ Three)+(SdS\ for\ Factor\ Four)+(SdS\ for\ Factor\ Five)}{5}$$

Your overall MLLQ index score can be interpreted using Table 5:

43

Table 5

Overall MLLQ Index Score

Above 600	VERY HIGH
571-600	HIGH
531-570	ABOVE AVERAGE
521-530	SLIGHTLY ABOVE AVERAGE
511-520	AVERAGE
486-510	SLIGHTLY BELOW AVERAGE
431-485	BELOW AVERAGE
371-430	LOW
Below 370	VERY LOW

The high-low ranking above can be further interpreted based on percentages within the normative sample. For example, if your school's overall MLLQ index was VERY HIGH then your school's developmentally responsive leadership score fell within 90% -100% of the normative sample. Interpretation of high-low rankings are as follows:

VERY HIGH	Above 89% of normative sample
HIGH	80-89% of normative sample
ABOVE AVERAGE	61-79% of normative sample
SLIGHTLY ABOVE AVERAGE	53-60% of normative sample
AVERAGE	48-52% of normative sample
SLIGHTLY BELOW AVERAGE	40-47% of normative sample
BELOW AVERAGE	20-39% of normative sample
LOW	10-19% of normative sample
VERY LOW	Below 10% of normative sample

Follow-Up Activities

Faculty and Staff

- Engage your faculty and staff in a discussion of the results.

Principal

- Reflect on the fact that principals tend to rate themselves more highly than teachers on instruments that measure instructional leadership.

Exemplar Middle School Practices Between Principals and Teachers

Part Three of the MLLQ involves an inventory of middle school practices and asks that the principal and teachers place a check next to the middle school components that are implemented in their school. In hopes of having people evaluate these items on the conservative side, a caveat regarding implementation is included that states "implemented in your school to an extent that you would invite others to observe them in action." It is important to note that no formal definitions of these middle school components are included on the MLLQ and that responses are based on what each respondent knows about these practices from studying such documents as *This We Believe: Successful Schools for Young Adolescents* (NMSA, 2003). It is also necessary to be cognizant of the fact that principals as a group tend to rate such items more highly than do teachers. As indicated in Table 6, principals rated exploratory curriculum; varied teaching and learning approaches; flexible scheduling; programs that promote health, wellness and safety; and team teaching higher than did the teachers. On the other hand, teachers ranked democratic governance, advisory programs, and the involvement of families and the community more highly.

The data obtained from this section of the MLLQ will provide rich information for a discussion about faculty and principal perceptions, permit a closer look at what each of the middle school practices involve, and result in a more complete implementation of these components in your school.

Although no statistically significant differences were found between principals' and teachers' perceptions of their school's exemplar middle school practices, the percentage differences between the two groups that did exist are interesting and noteworthy. These descriptive patterns are noted in Table 6.

Table 6

Exemplar Middle School Practices Reported by Principals and Teachers

Middle School Practices	Reported Percentages for Exemplary Practices	
	Principals	Teachers
Exploratory Curriculum	66.7%	43.0%
Varied Teaching and Learning Approaches	88.9%	83.7%
Flexible Scheduling	77.8%	51.4%
Democratic Governance of the School (with teachers, parents, community members)	22.2%	39.4%
Programs that Promote Health, Wellness, and Safety	77.8%	55.8%
Teaming	100.0%	78.1%
Advisory Programs	22.2%	48.2%
Involvement of Families and Communities	44.4%	58.2%

Mean Differences Between Principals and Teachers

Means and standard deviations were calculated for each factor (Table 7). The mean scores represent the average of all items (i.e., questions) associated with a given factor.

Table 7

Means and Standard Deviations

Factor	Principals' Mean Scores	Teachers' Mean Scores	Total Mean (principals and teachers)	Standard Deviation For Total Mean	t-test
One	4.46	4.25	4.26	.607	2.303*
Two	4.56	4.41	4.42	.678	1.587
Three	4.40	4.32	4.32	.641	.759
Four	4.03	3.72	3.73	.763	2.149
Five	4.56	4.05	4.07	.849	4.065**

*p<.05   **p<.01

In light of our incongruent group sample sizes (9 principals and 251 teachers), group differences were measured to determine distinctions between principals and teachers. Separate groups' t-tests were conducted to determine whether mean differences existed between principals and teachers for each factor. Statistically significant differences were found for Factor One, developmentally appropriate learning environment/support of teachers, $t(258) = 2.303$, $p < .05$ and for Factor Five, responsiveness to student needs/support of teachers, $t(258) = 4.065$, $p < .01$. Factor One showed that principals rated themselves higher on these questions (M = 4.46, SD = .248) than did the teachers (M = 4.25, SD = .615). Thus, principals perceive that they support teachers in providing for developmentally appropriate learning environments; but the teachers do not believe this as much as principals do. Principals also rated themselves higher for questions pertaining to Factor Five (M = 4.56, SD = .333) than did the teachers (M = 4.05, SD = .857). This indicates that principals believe they are providing responsiveness to student needs by supporting their teachers; and again, the teachers do not believe this notion as much as principals do. Overall, the results show that principals and teachers agree on responsiveness issues regarding student and school needs but not teacher needs.

Exemplar Middle School Practices

Results showed positive correlations between exemplar middle school practices and the construct factors. Principals and teachers associated particular middle school exemplar practices with distinct constructs regarding responsiveness to student, faculty, or schools needs. Both principals and teachers positively linked each factor with specific exemplar practices, with the exception of Factor Three, *developmentally appropriate learning environment/support of student needs*. Factor Three did not correlate with any of the eight middle school exemplar practices noted on the questionnaire. The other four factors with their associated exemplar practices are as follows:

Factor One—Developmentally Appropriate Learning Environment/Support of Teachers
a. Varied Teaching and Learning Approaches
b. Democratic Governance of the School (with teachers, parents, community)
c. Programs that Promote Good Health, Wellness, and Safety
d. Teaming
e. Advisory Programs
f. Involvement of Families and Communities

Factor Two—Best Practices
a. Exploratory Curriculum
b. Varied Teaching and Learning Approaches
c. Programs that Promote Good Health, Wellness, and Safety
d. Advisory Programs

Factor Four—Promote Student Self-Confidence and Competence
a. Varied Teaching and Learning Approaches
b. Democratic Governance of the School (with teachers, parents, community)
c. Involvement of Families and Communities

Factor Five—Responsiveness to Student Needs/Support of Teachers
a. Exploratory Curriculum
b. Flexible Scheduling

Follow-Up Activities

Faculty and Staff

- If not already done, engage your faculty and staff in a discussion of *This We Believe: Successful Schools for Young Adolescents* (NMSA, 2003). Have groups of faculty present each of the 14 characteristics of successful middle schools. Presentations could be scheduled for faculty meetings spanning the school year.

- Engage your faculty and staff in professional development activities using *Research and Resources in Support of* This We Believe (Anfara et al., 2003).

- Discuss the five factors and sub-scales that comprise the MLLQ (use Appendix A). Have your faculty brainstorm the kinds of activities a middle school principal can do to improve in each of these areas.

- Using the middle school practice inventory on the MLLQ instrument as a guide, discuss exemplary or non-exemplary middle school practices in your school.

Principal

- Reflect upon your knowledge of the characteristics of middle schools as delineated in *This We Believe: Successful Schools for Young Adolescents* (NMSA, 2003). Which areas do you most need to address with your faculty and staff?

- What district or state level impediments exist that affect your ability to create an exemplary middle school?

- Reflect on the mean differences in scores for Factors One and Five between principal and faculty. Were your results consistent with the results from the normative sample for both of these factors?

- Consider contributing the data derived from your implementation of the principal and teacher instruments to the ongoing research being conducted on developmentally responsive leadership, by contacting Vincent Anfara at vanfara@utk.edu. Your data will significantly help in the ongoing refinement of this instrument.

5. Conclusion

We noted in the introduction to this book that middle schools are under attack. Since the mid-1990s, there has been concern about the presumed "less than rigorous curriculum" found in middle schools. Middle schools have been characterized as "muddle in the middle," "a crack in the middle," and even "the wasteland of our educational landscape." Though these generalized judgments are not valid, they exist, nonetheless, and must be countered. We also acknowledged that the necessary attention has not been afforded to the middle school principal in the reform of middle schools.

In response to this realization, the Middle Level Education Research Special Interest Group (MLER-SIG) of the American Educational Research Association (AERA) endorsed a policy statement on middle school principal preparation and licensure. This group is comprised of the largest number of researchers dedicated to middle level issues that exists in the United States and internationally. In the group's policy brief (Anfara & Valentine, 2004), there is a call for preparation programs that include a focus on: (1) the unique needs and characteristics of young adolescents; (2) age-appropriate programs and practices used to promote the learning of young adolescents; (3) developmentally appropriate curriculum, instruction, and assessment of student learning; (4) middle school history and philosophy; and (5) the qualities and characteristics of effective middle level teachers and schools.

Related policy recommendations include: (1) states should establish mandatory requirements for future middle level administrators as an incentive for both colleges and universities and individuals to pursue specialization in middle level administration, (2) school districts and schools should require expertise in middle level issues and prior experience working with young adolescents in schools as prerequisites to being hired as a middle level administrator, and (3) states should require current middle level principals who have not had specialized middle level preparation to engage in graduate coursework or professional development in middle level issues.

We know what structures and components need to exist to establish a successful middle school (NMSA, 2003), but we have little idea of how the principal creates, implements, and sustains these structures and components in the process of creating a successful middle school. In short, one question remains. *Are middle level principals adequately prepared and professionally developed to effectively lead schools seeking to implement the middle school concept?*

Many principals are asking how and what questions. *How do I create highly effective and functional teacher teams? How do I get teachers, parents, and school district administrators to buy into exploratory curriculum and advisory programs? What do I do to improve student academic performance and promote their socioemotional growth? How do I effectively function as an instructional leader for middle level teachers?* It is our hope that the focused treatment of leadership together with the Middle Level Leadership Questionnaire (MLLQ) will afford middle level principals the opportunity to reflect on their behaviors and actions through the collection of data. These data can provide a meaningful snapshot assessment of one's developmental responsiveness as a middle level principal, and they can be used most effectively in a continuous data collection process aimed at the principal's professional growth and development that will lead to needed school improvement.

If, indeed, educational excellence is inextricably coupled with effective school leadership, there is much to be gained from studying the experience of school leaders. More specifically, given the need for additional research specific to middle school principals, the MLLQ provides us with the opportunity to learn from individuals as they live out their professional lives in middle schools.

Middle school principals who are serious about reforming their schools face a daunting challenge. They need to reconstruct core ideas about their role, and therefore, how they spend their time, set their priorities, seek new knowledge, refine skills, and situate themselves with respect to teachers, students, and others in the educational community. This process is complicated, takes time, and requires models of good practice.

Follow-Up Activities

Principal

- The process of collecting data about yourself can be a threatening experience. You have asked your teachers to evaluate one dimension of your leadership abilities. Reflect on this process. What have you learned about yourself that you did not know before? What did you know about yourself that was affirmed by this process?

- Reflect upon new behaviors that you plan to incorporate into your leadership repertoire. Create a list of these new behaviors for your periodic review.

- Explore other instruments (see Related Resources on p. 55) that are available that will provide you with data about your role as a middle school principal. As one example, The Organizational Health Inventory (OHI-M, Hoy & Tarter, 1997) will provide you with more information about your collegial leadership abilities (i.e., friendly, supportive, open, guided by norms of equality) and principal influence (i.e., ability to influence the action of superiors). The OHI-M is available at www.coe.ohio-state.edu/whoy/instruments_6.htm.

- Tie this data collection effort into your performance evaluation conducted by your school district or immediate supervisor.

References

Achilles, C. M. (1992). The leadership enigma is more than semantics. *Journal of School Leadership, 1*(1), 59-65.

Anfara, V. A., Jr., Andrews, P. G., Hough, D. L., Mertens, S. B., Mizelle, N. B., & White, G. P. (2003). *Research and resources in support of* This We Believe. Westerville, OH: National Middle School Association.

Anfara, V. A., Jr., & Brown, K. M. (2003). Voices from the middle: Preservice preparation and professional development of middle school principals. In P. G. Andrews & V. A. Anfara, Jr. (Eds.), *Leaders for a movement: Professional preparation and development of middle level teachers and administration* (pp. 203-222). Greenwich, CT: Information Age Publishing.

Anfara, V. A., Jr., Brown, K. M., Mills, R., Hartman, K. J., & Mahar, R. J. (2000, April). *Middle level leadership for the 21st century: Principals' views on essential skills and knowledge; Implications for successful preparation.* Paper presented at the annual meeting of the American Educational Research Association. New Orleans, LA.

Anfara, V. A., Jr., Patterson, F., Buehler, A., & Gearity, B. (2004, November). *School improvement planning in east Tennessee middle schools: A content analysis and perception study.* Paper presented at the annual conference of the National Middle School Association, Minneapolis, MN.

Anfara, V. A., Jr., Roney, K., Smarkola, C., & DuCette, J. (2003). *Middle level leadership questionnaire: Principal and teacher forms.* Knoxville, TN: Anfara & Associates.

Anfara. V. A., Jr., & Valentine, J. W. (2004). *Middle level principal preparation and licensure. A policy brief of the Middle Level Education Research Special Interest Group.* Retrieved November 30, 2004, from http://www.middlelevel.pdx.edu

Barnard, C. I. (1938). *Functions of the executive.* Cambridge, MA: Harvard University Press.

Barnard, C. I. (1948). *Organizations and management.* Cambridge, MA: Harvard University Press.

Bates, R. (1993). On knowing: Cultural and critical approaches to educational administration. *Educational Management and Administration, 21*(3), 171-176.

Bauck, J. (1987). Characteristics of the effective middle school principal. *NASSP Bulletin, 71*(500), 90-92.

Beck, L. (1994). *Reclaiming educational administration as a caring profession.* New York: Teachers College Press.

Bennis, W. G. (1983). *The chief.* New York: William Morrow.

Bennis, W. G., & Nanus, B. (1985). *Leaders: The strategies for taking charge.* New York: Harper & Row.

Bernhardt, V. A. (1998). *Data analysis for comprehensive schoolwide improvement.* Larchmont, NY: Eye on Education.

Blake, R. R., & Mouton, J. S. (1964). *The managerial grid.* Houston, TX: Gulf.

Bolman, L. G., & Deal, T. E. (1991). *Reframing organizations: Artistry, choice, and leadership.* San Francisco: Jossey-Bass.

Bradley, A. (1998, April 15). Muddle in the middle. *Education Week, 17* (31), 38-42.

Bradley, A., & Manzo, K. (2000, October 4). This weak link. *Education Week* (supplement), 3-8.

Brown, K. M., & Anfara, V. A., Jr. (2002). *From the desk of the middle school principal: Leadership responsive to the needs of young adolescents.* Lanham, MD: Scarecrow Press.

Brown, K. M., Anfara, V. A., Jr., & Gross. S. J. (2002). From the desk of the middle school principal. *Journal of School Leadership, 12*(4), 437-470.

Brown, K. M., Anfara, V. A., Jr., Hartman, K. J., Mahar, R. J., & Mills, R. (2001, April). *Professional development of middle level principals: Pushing the reform forward.* Paper presented at the annual meeting of the American Educational Research Association. Seattle, WA.

Burns, J. (1978). *Leadership.* New York: Harper & Row.

Carnegie Council on Adolescent Development. (1989). *Turning points: Preparing American youth for the 21st century.* New York: Carnegie Corporation.

Crawford, J. (1998). Changes in administrative licensure: 1991-1996. *UCEA Review, 39*(3), 8-10.

Cronin, T. E. (1993). Reflections on leadership. In W. E. Rosenbach & R. L. Taylor (Eds.), *Contemporary issues in leadership* (pp. 7-25). Boulder, CO: Westview Press.

Cunningham, W. G., & Gresso, D. W. (1993). *Cultural leadership: The culture of excellence in education.* Boston: Allyn & Bacon.

Deal, T. E., & Kennedy, A. (1982). *Corporate cultures*. Reading, MA: Addison-Wesley.

Duke, D. L. (1987). *School leadership and instructional improvement*. New York: Random House.

Duke, D. L. (1996). Perception, prescription and the future of school leadership. In K. Leithwood et al. (Eds.), *The international handbook of educational leadership and administration* (pp. 841-872). The Netherlands: Kluwer Academic Publishers.

Duke, D. L., & Leithwood, K. (1994). *Management and leadership: A comprehensive view of principals' functions*. Toronto: Ontario Institute for Studies in Education.

Dunning, G. (1993). Managing the small primary school: The problem role of the teaching head. *Educational Management and Administration, 21*(2), 79-89.

Eccles, J., & Midgley, C. (1989). Stage-environment fit: Developmentally appropriate classrooms for young adolescents. In R. E. Ames & C. Ames (Eds.), *Research on motivation in education* (Vol. 3, pp. 139-181). New York: Academic Press.

Eccles, J., Midgley, C., & Adler, T. (1984). Grade-related changes in school environment: Effects on achievement motivation. In J. H. Nicholls (Ed.), *The development of achievement motivation* (Vol.3, pp. 283-331). Greenwich, CT: JAI.

Enomoto, E. (1997). Schools as nested communities: Sergiovanni's metaphor extended. *Urban Education, 32*, 512-531.

Erikson, E. (1964). *Childhood and society*. New York: Norton.

Evers, C. W., & Lakomski, G. (1991). *Knowing educational administration: Contemporary methodological controversies in educational administration*. New York: Pergamon Press.

Fiedler, F. E. (1967). *A theory of leadership effectiveness*. New York: McGraw-Hill.

Finn, J. D. (1989). Withdrawing from school. *Review of Research, 59*, 117-143.

Foster, W. (1986). *Paradigms and promises: New approaches to educational administration*. Buffalo, NY: Prometheus Books.

Gardner, J. (1990). *On leadership*. New York: Free Press.

Gaskill, P. E. (2002). Progress in certification of middle level personnel. *Middle School Journal, 33*(5), 33-40.

George, P., & Grebing, W. (1992). Seven essential skills of middle level leadership. *Schools in the Middle, 1*(4), 3-11.

Greenfield, T. (1991). Re-forming and re-valuing educational administration: Whence and when cometh the phoenix? *Educational Management and Administration, 19*(4), 200-217.

Gross, S. J. (1998). *Staying centered: Curriculum leadership in a turbulent era*. Alexandria, VA: Association for Supervision and Curriculum Development.

Hallinger, P., & Murphy, J. (1985). Assessing the instructional management behavior of principals. *Elementary School Journal, 86*(2), 217-247.

Hankin, B., Abramson, L., Silva, P., McGee, R., Moffitt, T., & Angell, K. (1998). Development of depression from preadolescence to young adulthood: Emerging gender differences in a 10-year longitudinal study. *Journal of Abnormal Psychology, 107*, 128-140.

Harter, S. (1981). A new self-report scale of intrinsic versus extrinsic orientation in the classroom: Motivational and informational components. *Developmental Psychology, 17*, 300-312.

Hayes, D. (1995). The primary head's tale: Collaborative relationships in a timer of rapid change. *Educational Management and Administration, 23*(4), 233-244.

Hersey, P., & Blanchard, K. H. (1977). *Management of organizational behavior* (3rd ed.). Englewood Cliffs, NJ: Prentice-Hall.

Hodgkinson, C. (1991). *Educational leadership: The moral art*. Albany, NY: SUNY Press.

Hosford, P. L. (1984). The problem, its difficulties and our approaches. In P. L. Hosford (Ed.), *Using what we know about teaching*. Alexandria, VA: Association for Supervision and Curriculum Development.

Hoy, W. K., & Tarter, C. J. (1997). *The road to open and healthy schools: A handbook for change*. Thousand Oaks, CA: Corwin.

James, W. (1892). *Talks to teachers on psychology: And to students on some of life's ideals*. New York: Holt.

Jandris, T. P. (2001). *Data-based decision-making: Essential for principals*. Alexandria, VA: National Association of Elementary School Principals.

Leithwood, K. (1992). The move toward transformational leadership. *Educational Leadership, 49*(5), 8-12.

Leithwood, K. (1994). Leadership for school restructuring. *Educational Administration Quarterly, 30*(4), 498-518.

Leithwood, K. (1999). *Changing leadership for changing times*. Bristol, PA: Taylor Frances.

Leithwood, K., & Jantzi, D. (1999). The relative effects of principal and teacher sources of leadership on student engagement with school. *Educational Administration Quarterly, 35,* 679-706.

Leithwood, K., Steinbach, R., & Raun, T. (1993). Superintendents' group problem-solving processes. *Educational Administration Quarterly, 29*(3), 364-391.

Little, A. L., & Little, S. F. (2001). *How to become an exemplary middle school principal: A three step professional growth handbook*. Westerville, OH: National Middle School Association.

Manning, M. L. (1993). *Developmentally appropriate middle level schools*. Wheaton, MD: Association for Childhood Educational International.

Miller, A. C. (2000, April). *School reform in action*. Paper presented at the annual meeting of the American Educational Research Association, New Orleans, LA.

Murphy, J., & Hallinger, P. (1992). The principalship in an era of transformation. *Journal of Educational Administration, 30*(3), 77-88.

National Association for the Education of Young Children. (1997). *Statement of the position*. Retrieved April 17, 2006, from http://www.naeyc.org/about/positions/pdf/PSDAP98.PDF

National Middle School Association. (1982). *This we believe*. Columbus, OH: Author.

National Middle School Association. (2003). *This we believe: Successful schools for young adolescents*. Westerville, OH: Author.

Neuman, M., & Simmons, W. (2000). Leadership for student learning. *Phi Delta Kappan, 82*(1), 9-12.

Noddings, N. (2002). *Educating moral people: A caring alternative to character education*. New York: Teachers College Press.

Noddings, N. (1992). *The challenge to care in schools: An alternative approach to education*. New York: Teachers College Press.

North Central Regional Educational Laboratory. (2000). *Using data to bring about positive results in school improvement efforts*. Retrieved November 20, 2004, from: http://www.ncrel.org/toolbelt/tutor.htm

Olson, L. (2000). Policy focus converges on leadership: Several major new efforts under way. *Education Week, 19*(17), 1, 16-17.

Petersen, A., & Hamburg, B. (1986). Adolescence: A developmental approach to problems and psychopathology. *Behavior Therapy, 17,* 480-499.

Piaget, J. (1952). *The origins of intelligence in children*. New York: International Universities Press.

Sarason, S. B. (1996). *Barometers of change: Individual educational social transformation*. San Francisco: Jossey-Bass.

Sashkin, M., & Walberg, H. (1993). *Educational leadership and school culture*. Berkley, CA: McCutchan.

Schrag, F. (1978). The principal as a moral actor. In D. Erickson & T. Reller (Eds.), *The principal in metropolitan schools* (pp. 208-232). Berkley, CA: McCutchan.

Seyfarth, J. T. (1999). *The principal: New leadership for new challenges*. Upper Saddle River, NJ: Merrill.

Sergiovanni, T. J. (1996). *Leadership for the schoolhouse: How is it different? Why is it important?* San Francisco: Jossey-Bass.

Sergiovanni, T. J. (2001). *The principalship: A reflective practice perspective*. Boston: Allyn & Bacon.

Schein, E. (1985). *Organizational culture and leadership*. San Francisco: Jossey-Bass.

Schön, D. A. (1983). *The reflective practitioner: How professionals think in action*. New York: Basic Books.

Schön, D. A. (1987). *Educating the reflective practitioner*. San Francisco: Jossey-Bass.

Smith, W. F., & Andrews, R. L. (1989). *Instructional leadership: How principals make a difference*. Alexandria, VA: Association for Supervision and Curriculum Development.

Spillane, J., Halverson, R., & Diamond, J. (2001). Investigating school leadership practice: A distributed perspective. *Educational Researcher, 30*(3), 23-28.

Stack, C. (2003). *A passion for proof: Using data to accelerate student achievement*. Westerville, OH: National Middle School Association.

Stogdill, R. M. (1974). *Handbook of leadership: A survey of theory and research*. New York: The Free Press.

Tonnies, F. (1957). *Gemeinschaft unt Gessellschaft*. (Community and Society). (C. P. Loomis, Ed. and Trans.). New York: Harper-Collins.

Valentine, J. W., Clark, D. C., Hackman, D. G., Lucas, S. L., & Petzko, V. N. (2004). *A national study of leadership in middle level schools: Vol. 2. A national study of highly successful leaders and schools*. Reston, VA: National Association of Secondary School Principals.

Valentine, J. W., Clark, D. C., Hackman, D. G., & Petzko, V. N. (2002). *A national study of leadership in middle level schools: Vol. 1. A national study of middle level leaders and school programs.* Reston, VA: National Association of Secondary School Principals.

Valentine, J., Clark, D., Irvin, J., Keefe, J., & Melton, G. (1993). *Leadership in middle level education: Vol. 1. A national survey of middle level leaders in schools.* Reston, VA: National Association of Secondary School Principals.

Valentine, J., Clark, D., Nickerson, N., & Keefe, J. (1981). *The middle level principalship: Vol. 1. A survey of middle level principals and programs.* Reston, VA: National Association of Secondary School Principals.

Vygotsky, L. (1978). *Mind and society: The development of higher psychological processes.* Cambridge, MA: Harvard University Press.

Wade, H. H. (2001). *Data inquiry and analysis for educational reform.* (ERIC Document Reproduction Service No. ED 461911).

Weller, L. D. (1999). *Quality middle school leadership: Eleven central skill areas.* Lancaster, PA: Technomic Publishing.

Williamson, R., & Johnston, J. H. (1999). Challenging orthodoxy: An emerging agenda for middle level reform. *Middle School Journal, 30*(4), 10-17.

Related Resources

The following resources are offered to middle school principals for the dual purposes of school improvement and professional development. These references are divided into the following categories which parallel the topics discussed in this book: (1) using data for personal and school improvement, (2) instruments for collecting data in middle schools, (3) the principal as reflective practitioner, and (4) the middle school principal.

(1) Using Data for Personal and School Improvement

American Association of School Administrators. (2002). *Using data to improve schools: What's working.* Arlington, VA: Author. Retrieved March 29, 2006, from http://aasa.files.cms-plus.com/PDFs/Publications/UsingDataToImproveSchools.pdf

Ardovino, J., Hollingsworth, J., & Ybarra, S. (2000). *Multiple measures: Accurate ways to assess student achievement.* Thousand Oaks, CA: Corwin.

Bernhardt, V. L. (1994). *The school portfolio: A comprehensive framework for school improvement.* Larchmont, NY: Eye on Education.

Bernhardt, V. L. (1998). *Data analysis for comprehensive schoolwide improvement.* Larchmont, NY: Eye on Education.

Bernhardt, V. L. (2000). *Designing and using databases for school improvement.* Larchmont, NY: Eye on Education.

Bernhardt, V. L. (2002). *The school portfolio toolkit: A planning, implementation, and evaluation guide for continuous school improvement.* Larchmont, NY: Eye on Education.

Bernhardt, V. L. (2003). *Using data to improve student learning in elementary schools.* Larchmont, NY: Eye on Education.

Bernhardt, V. L., von Blanckensee, L. L., Lauck, M. S., Rebello, F. F., Bonilla, G. L., & Tribbey, M. M. (2000). *The example school portfolio—A companion to the school portfolio: A comprehensive framework for school improvement.* Larchmont, NY: Eye on Education.

Converse, J. M., & Presser, S. (1986). *Survey questions: Handcrafting the standardized questionnaire.* Beverly Hills, CA: Sage.

Creighton, T. B. (2001). *Schools and data: The educator's guide for using data to improve decision making.* Thousand Oaks, CA: Corwin.

Doyle, D. P., & Pimentel, S. (1997). *Raising the standard: An eight-step action guide for schools and communities.* Thousand Oaks, CA: Corwin.

Fink, A., & Kosecoff, J. B. (1998). *How to conduct surveys: A step-by-step guide* (2nd ed.). Newbury Park, CA: Sage.

Fitzpatrick, K. A. (1997). *Indicators of schools of quality: A research-based self-assessment guide for schools committed to continuous improvement.* Schaumburg, IL: National Study of School Evaluation.

Herman, J., & Winters, L. (1992). *Tracking your school's success: A guide to sensible evaluation.* Newbury Park, CA: Sage.

Holcomb, E. L. (1999). *Getting excited about data: How to combine people, passion, and proof.* Thousand Oaks, CA: Corwin.

Johnson, R. S. (2002). *Using data to close the achievement gap: How to measure equity in our schools.* Thousand Oaks, CA: Corwin.

Leibowitz, M. (1999). *Promoting learning through student data.* Alexandria, VA: Association for Supervision and Curriculum Development.

LeTendre, B., & Lipka, R. P. (1999). *Getting answers to your questions: A middle-level educator's guide to program evaluation.* Norwood, MA: Christopher-Gordon.

Levesque, K., Brady, D., Rossi, K., & Teitelbaum, P. (1998). *At your fingertips: Using everyday data to improve schools.* Berkeley, CA: MPR Associates.

Love, N. (2002). *Using data/getting results: A practical guide for school improvement in mathematics and science.* Norwood, MA: Christopher-Gordon.

National Association of Elementary School Principals (NAESP). (2001). Standard five: Use multiple sources of data as diagnostic tools. In NAESP, *Leading learning communities: Standards for what principals should know and be able to do* (pp. 55-66). Alexandria, VA: Author.

Schmoker, M. (1999). *Results: The key to continuous school improvement* (2nd ed.). Alexandria, VA: Association for Supervision and Curriculum Development.

Wagner, M., Fiester, L., Reisner, E., Murphy, D., & Golan, S. (1997). *Making information work for you: A guide to collecting good information and using it to improve comprehensive strategies for children, families, and communities.* Washington, DC: U.S. Department of Education.

(2) Instruments for Collecting Data in Middle Schools

National Staff Development Council. (2003). *Test your professional development IQ. Tools for Schools.* Available online at www.nsdc.org/library/publications/tools/tools8-03pdiq.cfm

Venture Philanthropy Partners. (n.d.). *McKinsey capacity assessment grid.* Available online at www.emcf.org/pdf/mckinsey_capacitytool.pdf

In addition to the Middle Level Leadership Questionnaire (MLLQ) developed by Anfara, Roney, Smarkola, and DuCette (2003), the following instruments are available for use in middle schools. Many of these instruments were designed specifically for middle school application. Some of these instruments are free for your use; others have costs associated with their use. Those interested in using these instruments are encouraged to contact the developers before proceeding.

Available from the Middle Level Leadership Center (instruments are available for your review on the Web site, www.mllc.org

(1)   Instructional Practices Survey (IPS)—developed by the Middle Level Leadership Center, University of Missouri, Columbia
(2)   School Culture Survey (SCS)—developed by Steve Gruenert and Jerry Valentine
(3)   Middle Level Student Survey—developed by Jerry Valentine and David Dubois

Available from Wayne Hoy at The Ohio State University, www.coe.ohio-state.edu/whoy/instruments_6.htm

These instruments are available free of charge, and all information pertaining to the instruments, their use, and scoring is available at the Web site. Those interested in using any of the following instruments are encouraged to contact Dr. Hoy via e-mail at Hoy.16@osu.edu.

(1)   Organizational Climate Description Questionnaire for Middle (OCDQ-M)
(2)   Organizational Health Inventory for Middle (OHI-M)
(3)   Pupil Control Ideology Form (PCI)
(4)   Trust Scales (T-Scale)
(5)   Omnibus T-Scale (Omnibus T-Scale)
(6)   Organizational Climate Index (OCI)
(7)   Teacher Sense of Efficacy
(8)   Collective Efficacy (CE-Scale)
(9)   Enabling School Structure (ESS)
(10)   Organizational Citizenship Behavior Scale (OCB)
(11)   School Mindfulness Scale (M-Scale)
(12)   Organizational Justice Scale (OJ-Scale)

(3) The Principal as Reflective Practitioner

Brown, G., & Irby, B. (1995). The portfolio: Should it be used by administrators? *NASSP Bulletin, 79*(570), 82-85.

Fulmer, C. (1993). Developing a reflective practice of professional development. *Business Affairs, 59*(9), 23-26.

Johnson, S. M. (1990). *Teachers at work: Achieving success in our schools.* New York: Basic Books.

North Carolina Department of Public Instruction. (n.d.). Self-assessment: The reflective practitioner. Retrieved January 10, 2006, from http://www.ncpublicschools.org/pbl/pblreflect.htm

Richardson, J. (2002). Reflection gives educators a chance to tap into what they've learned. *Tools for Schools.* Retrieved January 10, 2006, from http://www.nsdc.org/library/publications/tools/tools4-02rich.cfm

Schön, D. A. (1983). *The reflective practitioner: How professionals think in action.* New York: Basic Books.

Schön, D. A. (1984). Leadership as reflection in action. In T. J. Sergiovanni & J. E. Corbally (Eds.), *Leadership and organizational culture* (pp. 64-72). Urbana-Champaign, IL: University of Illinois Press.

Schön, D. A. (1987). *Educating the reflective practitioner.* San Francisco: Jossey-Bass.

Sergiovanni, T. J. (1991). *The principalship: A reflective practice perspective.* Boston: Allyn & Bacon.

Short, P., & Rinehart, R. (1993). Reflection as a means of developing expertise. *Educational Administration Quarterly, 29*(4), 501-521.

Willower, D. (1994). Dewey's theory of inquiry and reflective administration. *Journal of Educational Administration, 32*(1), 5-22.

(4) The Middle School Principal

Anfara, V. A., Jr., Brown, K. M., Mills, R., Hartman, K., & Mahar, R. J. (2001). Middle level leadership for the 21st century. In V. A. Anfara, Jr. (Ed.), *The handbook of research in middle level education* (pp. 183-213). Greenwich, CT: Information Age Publishing.

Bauck, J. (1987). Characteristics of the effective middle school principal, *NASSP Bulletin, 71*(500), 90-92.

Brown, K. M., & Anfara, V. A., Jr. (2002). *From the desk of the middle school principal: Leadership responsive to the needs of young adolescents.* Lanham, MD: Scarecrow Press.

Curtis, D. (2002). *The freshman principal. Edutopia.* The George Lucas Educational Foundation. Retrieved January 10, 2006, from http://www.edutopia.org/php/article.php?id=Art_1000

Doda, N., & Williamson, R. (2002). Principals make a difference: Learning and leading together. In N. Doda & S. Thompson (Eds.), *Transforming ourselves, transforming schools* (pp. 279-292). Westerville, OH: National Middle School Association.

George, P., & Grebing, W. (1992). Seven essential skills of middle level leadership. *Schools in the Middle, 1*(4), 3-11.

Gross, S. J. (2003). Leadership standards or leaving standardization for leadership? What best meets the needs of a middle level movement during times of severe turbulence? In P. G. Andrews & V. A. Anfara, Jr. (Eds.), *Leaders for a movement: Professional preparation and development of middle level teachers and administration* (pp. 179-201). Greenwich, CT: Information Age Publishing.

Glatthorn, A. A., & Spencer, N. K. (1986). *Middle school/junior high principal's handbook: A practical guide for developing better schools.* Englewood Cliffs, NJ: Prentice-Hall.

Little, A. L., & Little, S. F. (2001). *How to become an exemplary middle school principal: A three step professional growth handbook.* Westerville, OH: National Middle School Association.

Mizell, M. H. (1994). The new principal. *The Hayes Mizell Reader.* Available online at http://www.middleweb.com/Newprincipal.html

Mizell, M. H. (1995). Looking for leaders. *The Hayes Mizell Reader.* Available online at http://www.middleweb.com/Lookingldrs.html

Mizell, M. H. (2002). *Shooting for the sun: The message of middle school reform.* New York: The Edna McConnell Clark Foundation. Book available online at http://www.nsdc.org/library/authors/shootingsun.pdf

Petzko, V. N. (2003). Support for new and experienced middle level principals: A proposed model for professional development. In P. G. Andrews & V. A. Anfara, Jr. (Eds.), *Leaders for a movement: Professional preparation and development of middle level teachers and administration* (pp. 223-247). Greenwich, CT: Information Age Publishing.

Valentine, J. W., Clark, D. C., Hackman, D. G., Lucas, S. L., & Petzko, V. N. (2004). A national study of leadership in middle level schools: Vol. 2. A national study of highly successful leaders and schools. Reston, VA: National Association of Secondary School Principals.

Valentine, J. W., Clark, D. C., Hackman, D. G., & Petzko, V. N. (2002). *A national study of leadership in middle level schools: Vol. 1. A national study of middle level leaders and school programs.* Reston, VA: National Association of Secondary School Principals.

Valentine, J., Clark, D., Irvin, J., Keefe, J., & Melton, G. (1993). *Leadership in middle level education: Vol. 1. A national survey of middle level leaders in schools.* Reston, VA: National Association of Secondary School Principals.

Valentine, J., Clark, D., Nickerson, N., & Keefe, J. (1981). *The middle level principalship: Vol. 1. A survey of middle level principals and programs.* Reston, VA: National Association of Secondary School Principals.

Weller, L. D. (1999). Quality middle school leadership: Eleven central skill areas. Lancaster, PA: Technomic.

Williamson, R., & Galletti, S. (2003). Leadership for results. In P. G. Andrews & V. A. Anfara, Jr. (Eds.), *Leaders for a movement: Professional preparation and development of middle level teachers and administration* (pp. 271-298). Greenwich, CT: Information Age Publishing.

Appendix A

Instrument Development

A pilot group of 45 middle level experts and principals provided feedback on the original 65-item instrument for content validity purposes. This group was asked to comment on the extent of importance (*very, somewhat, not*) and clarity (*clear, not clear*) of each item. Group comments were coded and entered into SPSS, a statistical software package. Two reports were generated from SPSS to assist in the decision to retain, modify, or eliminate an item. Each report ranked the items in order of their importance and clarity. It was found that the two different SPSS rank reporting methods produced similar results. Based on these rankings, 32 questions were eliminated, leaving a 33-item, 5-response (*frequently, if not always; fairly often; sometimes; once in a while; not at all*) Likert-scale instrument. All of the negatively worded statements were removed as part of this process.

The resulting questionnaire was administered to the principals and teachers in nine schools. The instrument consists of two forms—a principal's form and a teacher's form. Completed questionnaires were received from the nine principals and their teachers (251) currently working in middle schools in Pennsylvania and Tennessee. The principal's form documents principals' ratings of their own behaviors relevant to middle school practices, while the teacher's form documents teachers' ratings of their principal's behaviors towards these same practices.

To provide construct validity of the instrument, a factor analysis and scale reliability test was performed on the returned responses. A principal axis factoring analysis with varimax rotation was executed on the questionnaire items for both the principals and teachers. The factor analysis rendered five constructs: (1) developmentally appropriate learning environment/support of teachers, (2) best practices, (3) developmentally appropriate learning environment/support of student needs, (4) promote student self-confidence and competence, and (5) responsiveness to student needs/support of teachers (see Appendix A for a description of each factor). The five construct factors fit within the original three-part model (i.e. responsiveness to student, faculty, and school needs) of the developmentally responsive middle level leader developed by Brown, Anfara, and Gross (2002). Factors One and Five correspond to responsiveness to faculty, Factor Two is associated with the responsiveness to school needs, and Factors Three and Four relate to responsiveness to students. Of the 35-items used for the factor analysis, two questions did not fit within a factor construct and were deleted from the questionnaire. Consequently, the final version of the Middle Level Leadership Questionnaire (MLLQ) contained in this book consists of 33 items.

Reliability was measured by determining the internal consistency (alpha coefficient) of items within each factor. The alpha coefficients for Factors One through Five, respectively, are .93, .89, .81, .76, and .72. Overall, the reliability scores for these subscales ranged from moderate to high.

Appendix B

Factor Analysis Definitions

Factor One:
Developmentally Appropriate Learning Environment/Support of Teachers

The developmentally responsive middle level principal helps teachers in the creation of a learning environment that addresses students' affective and cognitive needs. This includes encouraging teachers to provide students with opportunities to explore, make mistakes, and grow in a safe, caring environment; encouraging active, discovery learning; and offering special interest classes.

Factor Two:
Best Practices

The developmentally responsive middle level principal understands the middle school philosophy and implements it through best practices like advisory and transition programs as well as varied instructional approaches.

Factor Three:
Developmentally Appropriate Learning Environment/ Support of Student Needs

The developmentally responsive middle level principal makes decisions based on the needs of young adolescents and supports students by providing opportunities to examine options of behavior and their resulting consequences.

Factor Four:
Promotes Student Self-Confidence and Competence

The developmentally responsive middle level principal supports students in making connections to achieve self-confidence and competence through spending time with students; allowing them to explore topics and demonstrate competence; and viewing students as important participants in planning and program development.

Factor Five:
Responsiveness to Student Needs/Support of Teachers

The developmentally responsive middle level principal provides teachers with time for planning and encourages modifications of time, grouping, and instructional strategies to meet students' needs.

About the Authors

Vincent A. Anfara, Jr. is associate professor and program coordinator of educational administration at The University of Tennessee, Knoxville. He is currently chair of the National Middle School Association's Research Advisory Board and past president of the Middle Level Education Research Special Interest Group of the American Educational Research Association.

Kathleen Roney is assistant professor of curricular studies at The University of North Carolina Wilmington. She currently serves as president of the Middle Level Education Research Special Interest Group of the American Educational Research Association.

Claudia Smarkola received her doctoral degree in educational psychology from Temple University, Philadelphia, PA. Her specialty areas include instructional technology and statistics. She currently works as a research associate at Mid-Atlantic Regional Educational Laboratory at Temple University Center for Research in Human Development and Education.

Joseph P. DuCette is professor of educational psychology at Temple University in Philadelphia, and his research is focused on program evaluation, statistics, and attribution theory. He served the College of Education for many years as its senior associate dean.

Steven J. Gross is associate professor of educational leadership and policy studies at Temple University, Philadelphia, PA. His research centers on initiating and sustaining deep innovation in education and the development of turbulence theory. He is a senior fellow at the Vermont Society for the Study of Education.

National Middle School Association

National Middle School Association, established in 1973, is the voice for professionals and others interested in the education and well-being of young adolescents. The association has grown rapidly and enrolls members in all 50 states, the Canadian provinces, and 46 other nations. In addition, 58 state, regional, and provincial middle school associations are official affiliates of NMSA.

NMSA is the only national association dedicated exclusively to the education, development, and growth of young adolescents. Membership is open to all. While middle level teachers and administrators make up the bulk of the membership, central office personnel, college and university faculty, state department officials, other professionals, parents, and lay citizens are members and active in supporting our single mission —improving the educational experiences of 10- to 15-year-olds. One of NMSA's particular strengths is its open and diverse membership.

The association publishes *Middle School Journal,* the movement's premier professional journal; *Research in Middle Level Education Online; Middle Ground, the Magazine of Middle Level Education; The Family Connection,* an online newsletter for families; *Classroom Connections,* a practical quarterly resource; and a series of research summaries.

A leading publisher of professional books in the field of middle level education, NMSA provides resources both for understanding and advancing various aspects of the middle school concept and for assisting classroom teachers in planning for instruction. More than 150 NMSA publications are available through the resource catalog as well as selected titles published by other organizations.

The association's highly acclaimed annual conference attracts nearly 10,000 attendees every fall. NMSA also sponsors many other professional development opportunities.

For information about NMSA and its many services, contact the association's headquarters office at 4151 Executive Parkway, Suite 300, Westerville, Ohio, 43081. Tel ephone: 800-528-NMSA; Fax: 614-895-4750; Web sit e: www.nmsa.org.